PSL LIBRARY OF OCEAN TRAVEL

# THE ROMANCE OF A MODERN LINER

*by*

## CAPTAIN E. G. DIGGLE, RD RNR

### WITH A NEW FOREWORD BY
## CHARLES HAAS

PATRICK STEPHENS LIMITED

THE "AQUITANIA" IN A FAMILIAR SETTING AT SOUTHAMPTON

Frontispiece]

# THE ROMANCE OF
# A MODERN LINER

BY

## CAPTAIN E. G. DIGGLE, R.D., R.N.R.

*Commander of R.M.S. AQUITANIA*

*WITH A FOREWORD BY*

ADMIRAL OF THE FLEET
### EARL JELLICOE OF SCAPA
### O.M., G.C.B., G.C.V.O.

PATRICK STEPHENS LIMITED

First published in about 1930 by
Sampson Low, Marston & Co Ltd.
This edition first published 1989

British Library Cataloguing in Publication Data

Diggle, E.G.
The romance of a modern liner.—(PSL library
of ocean travel).
1. Cruises by liners, history
I. Title
910.4'5

ISBN 1-85260-168-X

*Patrick Stephens Limited is part of the
Thorsons Publishing Group,
Wellingborough, Northamptonshire, NN8 2RQ, England*

Printed in Great Britain by
The Bath Press, Bath, Avon

1   3   5   7   9   10   8   6   4   2

# PUBLISHER'S PREFACE

The *PSL Library of Ocean Travel* is a collection of significant books on ships and the sea, long out-of-print but now re-issued in facsimile editions.

All the books to be included in the Library — each of which has been selected by members of a 'panel' of distinguished maritime authors and collectors — have been chosen for the rarity of their original editions, for the authoritativeness of the writer, and, above all, for their readability. Autobiographies, biographies, histories of famous ships of the past and the reminiscences of eminent mariners and sea travellers are all included, and will have a wide appeal to the thousands of present-day ship enthusiasts who have a deep interest in the maritime history of the past hundred years. For the majority of such readers, these books may be unknown and would otherwise be entirely unobtainable.

Many of the original volumes used in the production of these new editions have been supplied by Mainmast Books, of Saxmundham, Suffolk, IP17 1HZ, England, from whom all volumes in the *PSL Library of Ocean Travel* may be obtained.

*The Romance of a Modern Liner* by Captain E. G. Diggle, originally published in about 1930 by Sampson Low, Marston & Co, is the third volume in the *PSL Library of Ocean Travel*, and the publishers would like to thank Charles Haas for providing a foreword for this facsimile edition. Finally, please note that while all the illustrations from the original edition are included, they have been gathered together rather than distributed through the text. Also, four of the pictures, originally in colour, have had to be rendered in monochrome in the present edition.

# ACKNOWLEDGMENT

CAPTAIN DIGGLE acknowledges the valuable assistance of Kenneth J. Redwood, George E. Champion, Allen Whitmore and T. E. Hughes, of the Cunard Steam Ship Company, Limited, in the compilation of this book.

This acknowledgment will be sufficient explanation of the appearance of Captain Diggle's name in the text.

PSL LIBRARY OF OCEAN TRAVEL

Also available

*Mauretania*
by Humfrey Jordan

*Tramps and Ladies*
by Sir James Bisset

*A Million Ocean Miles*
by Sir Edgar T. Britten

Other titles in preparation

*The Ocean Tramp*
by Frank C. Hendry

*Atlantic Ferry*
by Arthur J. Maginnis

*Sail Ho!*
by Sir James Bisset

Patrick Stephens Limited will always be pleased to hear of any titles which are felt to be worthy for possible inclusion in the *PSL Library of Ocean Travel* in the future.

# FOREWORD
## to this new edition by
## Charles Haas

*Aquitania* — the Grand Old Lady of the Atlantic. Proud survivor of two world wars. A means of transportation, but so much more: the embodiment of a world, a people and a different time.

Few ships have enjoyed the public adoration and patronage *Aquitania* experienced in her 35 years of service. At the time of her maiden voyage, human flight was just 11 years old and wireless was still something of a novelty. By the time of her retirement, jet aircraft and television were household words. Within this span, *Aquitania* compiled a record of safety and comfort that few ships could match.

Yet, somehow, the great liner's successes seemed overshadowed by other events. Consistency and safety are not the stuff of which headlines are made. Her quest for a public following was terminated abruptly after three voyages when World War I intervened. Some of her contemporaries — *Titanic*, *Lusitania*, *Normandie* — became better known through tragic endings, while others were immortalized in record books for size or speed.

Fortunately for those who love the sea and great ships, *Aquitania* was to have a knowledgeable biographer in the person of one of her captains, Ernest Granville Diggle, given command of the great vessel in 1929. *The Romance of a Modern Liner*, published about a year later, is a stirring portrait in words and pictures of this immortal ship.

Fortunately for the reader, Diggle's book is not a dry, statistics-laden tome — even though there are plenty of fascinating facts to enjoy — but a personal tour of the ship from her design and launch to her daily operation. We are taken behind the scenes to see the miracle of ocean travel: the crew who make it possible and the facilities of a city at sea.

*The Romance of a Modern Liner* is an aptly named love song to a gracious lady. At the time of her retirement in 1950, Cunard chairman F. A. Bates said of *Aquitania*, 'In peace and war, fair weather and foul, she has done her duty in a manner unsurpassed by any other of her sisters who have helped to build up the Company's long history. With all truth it can be said, "She did well to the end", and that must be the thought of all who have sailed in, or served with her.' Captain Diggle's book tells us the 'how' and the 'why'.

CHARLES HAAS
New Jersey, USA
Co-author, *Titanic: Triumph and Tragedy*
and *Titanic: Destination Disaster*

# FOREWORD

*by*

ADMIRAL OF THE FLEET
EARL JELLICOE OF SCAPA
O.M., G.C.B., G.C.V.O.

IF we are to have in future only a comparatively small Navy, it is all the more important that the nation should realise the essential contribution which the Merchant Navy makes to their sea sea prestige, and the strength of the British peoples, The two services are complementary the one to the other. There was a time, of course, when there was no division between ships of war and ships of commerce. In the days of the Armada, and even in later wars, down to the beginning of the nineteenth century, the Royal Navy had to be very strongly reinforced in time of war by ships belonging to private traders or trading corporations. In subsequent years the breach widened, but in 1914 again we saw the British Mercantile Marine acting in the closest touch with the Royal Navy; indeed the Royal Navy could not have fulfilled its mission if it had not had the support of the Merchant Navy, of which the Prince of Wales is now the Master. No ship was too humble or ancient not to be required. Trawlers and drifters, the small traders, the tramp steamer, the private yacht, and the palatial liner were all called into service, and the public were thrilled at the scanty rumours that leaked through of the valiant exploits of armed merchant cruisers, mine-sweepers, and patrol vessels.

The interest aroused in the Merchant Service during the Great War still continues, and of all classes of ships the one that has perhaps the most universal appeal is the great liner. With its four massive funnels and gigantic hull, which carries some 4,000 persons in one trip across the Atlantic, a ship like the *Aquitania*, the largest liner built in Great Britain, or the world-famous *Mauretania*, is surely not only a triumph of the shipbuilders' craft, but also the embodiment of efficient organisation and service.

It is sometimes said that the modern liner sailor is not a sailor any more. Modern machinery and inventions have, of course, developed to an enormous extent, with the object of rendering travel at sea as safe as on land. But consider the responsibilities of the captain of a huge Atlantic liner. He has the safety of some thousands of lives in his hands, and a ship worth between three and four millions. Modern progress has not abolished storms, fogs, icebergs, uncharted rocks, unsuspected and other dangers. And do not forget that this responsibility continues for voyage after voyage, fair weather or foul, with little respite year after year. It is a responsibility that could not possibly be borne without changed and improved modern conditions. And the infrequency of accidents, which is a striking characteristic of the line to which the *Aquitania* belongs, is surely a tribute to the efficiency and devotion of the mercantile marine branch of the British sea service. It is only because its discipline is of the highest, and its sense of responsibility particularly strong, that it has attained to and maintained for so long the foremost position amongst the fleets of the maritime nations of the world.

# CONTENTS

# ILLUSTRATIONS

# ILLUSTRATIONS

# THE ROMANCE
# OF A MODERN LINER

## CHAPTER I

### PLANNING AND CONSTRUCTION

In these days of television, talkie films, and aeroplanes speeding at hundreds of miles an hour, we are rather apt to accept wonders as a matter of everyday occurrence, and it is very remarkable that an ocean liner should continue to hold the admiration of the public as it does to-day. To the British boy it suggests, and quite rightly, a great wealth of romance. It is fortunate for us as a nation that it should make such an appeal in this way. In our island story there are no brighter pages than those that deal with British ships and British sailors. There has grown up during the past centuries a tradition of the sea, not merely a tradition of the Royal Navy, but an equally glorious tradition of the Merchant Service. Most

of its work is done in silence, but its vital importance to the prosperity of the nation and the
Empire cannot be over-estimated. The Elizabethan period was certainly one of the most
glorious of all, but those qualities which distinguished the sea-dogs of Devon are just as
prominent to-day—they are loyalty, fearlessness
and self-sacrifice. These are the qualities which
have always distinguished, and which still distinguish, the members of that great brotherhood
of "those who go down to the sea in ships."
Steamers are not the least romantic part of the
whole story of ships and the sea, and it is the
Atlantic ferry which is invested with the greatest
romance in the mind of thousands of people, the
majority of whom have never crossed the ocean in
their lives.

In these sea-girt isles our fortunes, of course,
do not so much depend upon the liners as upon
those inconspicuous cargo ships up and down
the seven salt seas, but the North Atlantic—the
big and fast steamer route—is fixed in the
popular imagination by a succession of notable,
historic, and, romantic events. Owing to the
number of competing lines of all nations and
the comparative shortness of the voyage, the
North Atlantic has always been the chief centre
of rivalry and the route on which the best ships

for speed, size, and luxury have always been found.

Much has been written about steamships in a general kind of way, but in this book it is intended to give you the life story of one of the greatest liners in the world—the *Aquitania*.

The chief object of the book is to show something of the many stages and processes through which this great ocean-going liner had to pass, from the time of laying the keel right up to the present day.

She is known as the "world's wonder ship," and is a steamer of which everyone might well be proud, not only on account of her great size, but because she represents the highest achievement of British skill and workmanship. She has earned enduring fame on account of the perfect scheme of her construction and equipment, and the artistic arrangement of her accommodation. In her massive frame, which in length is just a little longer than the Tower Bridge of London, are contained hundreds of British inventions representing the vast experience of the finest naval architects and marine engineers in the world.

The *Aquitania* embarked upon her actual career in May, 1914, and made three voyages to New York from Liverpool prior to being taken over by the Government on the outbreak of the Great War in 1914. After being converted into an armed cruiser carrying six-inch guns, she left the river Mersey for patrol duty on August 8, 1914, just four days after the declaration of war, a remarkable achievement, considering the alterations which had to be made.

In May, 1915, she was converted to a transport, and between this date and August carried some 30,000 troops to the Dardanelles. She then became a hospital ship until the end of 1916, and carried a total of no fewer than 25,000 wounded troops. Early in 1918 she was again requisitioned as a transport, and made nine trips across the Atlantic, carrying over 60,000 American troops to Europe. Upwards of 120,000 troops were, in fact, carried by the *Aquitania* during her war service.

Immediately the war was over she was engaged in carrying tens of thousands of Canadian and American soldiers back across the Atlantic, and then followed the peaceful career for which she was intended—of carrying passengers to New York, and this duty she has carried out faithfully since.

It was in December, 1910, that the order for building the *Aquitania* was placed by the Cunard Steam Ship Company with Messrs. John Brown

& Co., Ltd., of Clydebank. Now the problems that call for consideration before an order is placed for the construction of a big steamer are tremendous. The first point is—what is to be the service in which she is to be run, and what is to be her purpose? Is she to be solely for carrying passengers? Is she to carry passengers as well as freight, or freight only? These important points govern the size of the ship, the speed at which she is to be propelled, the number of passengers she is to carry, what proportions are to be allocated to the various classes of accommodation, whether there are to be very luxurious furnishings and decorations or those of plain and simple comfort, whether the carriage of cargo or freight is to be of any great consideration, and, if so, how much.

It will be realised that this early stage is therefore one of the utmost concern and importance, and demands much careful thought by both owners and builders.

In the case of the *Aquitania*, the carriage of freight is more or less a secondary consideration, as she was to be essentially a carrier of passengers on a sort of ferry, at a speed which will enable them to travel from one side of the Atlantic to the other in less than a week. To achieve this object, therefore, a speed of from 22 to 23 knots was considered essential. Her average sea speed, as a matter of fact, is in the neighbourhood of 23 knots. With favourable weather conditions she has done 23½ to 24 knots which shows, therefore, that she has a good reserve of power for use in emergency or levelling up in the passage should bad weather be encountered.

Of course there have been, and there are, steamers which are faster than the *Aquitania*, such as the *Mauretania*, which has reached 30 knots in the English Channel, and 27½ on the Atlantic. The latter, however, was built with that specific purpose in view.

The speed of the liner having been decided, the next step was to ascertain the size which would best contain the engines and machinery for developing the horse-power necessary to obtain this speed, along with a capacity for carrying fuel for the Atlantic voyage together with a reserve.

In working out the space for the bedrooms, public rooms, promenades, and generally the area to be occupied by the passengers, what has to be kept in mind is whether this can be made economical and commercially successful. In other words, the money obtained from the passengers must be sufficient not only to pay the expenses of running the ship but also to provide a good margin to meet costs ashore and so on.

Passenger traffic across the Atlantic is of a very fluctuating character. There are periods, all too short, from the owners' point of view, when the tonnage is insufficient to carry the passengers, and, on the other hand, there are long periods when the number of passengers moving is so small that ships have to be laid up or some other use found for them. This is in the winter, of course, and it explains why quite a number of Atlantic liners to-day are utilised for cruises round the world, in the Mediterranean and elsewhere.

In constructing the *Aquitania* the Cunard Company felt that if they provided a ship which would carry as a maximum about 750 first-class, 600 second, and from 1,500 to 2,000 third-class passengers, and a crew of about 800 to 900, in all a total of something like 3,500 people, they would have gauged her capacity fairly accurately.

It must be remembered, however, that the present United States quota restrictions were not then in force. On account of these restrictions, and the consequent loss of business, the steamship lines have had to seek other sources of traffic. This explains chiefly how the new class—tourist third cabin has come into vogue.

The *Aquitania* now has accommodation for over 250 tourist third cabin passengers, and, in order to provide the necessary space, a considerable rearrangement of her original plan of accommodation had to be carried out. This new accommodation has been designed to provide comfortable accommodation at a low cost, and so bring the pleasures of an Atlantic crossing within the reach of holiday-makers and people who are not looking for luxury, but want to get a chance of seeing the New World. Incidentally, it has been done in such a way as to relieve the traveller of certain vexatious steerage regulations and immigration laws.

The management of the company, having decided upon these essential points, then placed them before their naval architect and his staff to work out a draft of the proposed ship. But before this could be done the varied and very conflicting requirements of the various people ashore who superintend the departments of the ship, had to be studied—the marine department concerned with the navigation of the ship, the engineering and catering departments, as well as the passenger and freight departments. Also there were numerous rules and regulations of the Board of Trade and classification societies in connection with the strength of girders, framing, sub-division of the ship, provision of boats, davits and all those important things concerned with the stability and safety of the ship. Furthermore, it had to be ensured that the ship should be of pleasing appearance.

She had also to be given a pleasing name. For precisely the same reason that a good trade name is necessary for a commercial product, a shipping company must provide a good name for a ship. In making a selection from probably a hundred or more suggestions, consideration has to be given both to the sound and general suggestiveness of the name. There is a very old phrase "Give a dog a bad name," but just imagine the result of giving a bad name to a ship. A good name, however, has little power to propagate itself. It must be established in the minds of the general public by successful advertising. The names of the *Aquitania* and *Mauretania* are, perhaps, more familiar to the world than any other ship. Although this is to some extent the result of effective propaganda, the merits of these liners have been the chief means of enhancing their popularity.

Practically all the shipping companies have adopted a specific formula for the names of their ships. One line has chosen the idea of naming them after the great personages in ecclesiastical history. Another line has ships, the names of which are identified by the great cities of the world, others by the names of stars and shells. There are the Castle boats, Port ships and Saints' ships. Some names are prefixed by the words Manchester, Santa, Fort and so on. Another big Atlantic liner company adopts a suffix "ic" as the ending of names which have geographical association. It will be seen by looking at the names of the liners under the heading "Cunard" that they all have the suffix "ia," and have been named after provinces in the ancient Roman empire. There are a few exceptions to the rule; one for example, is the mammoth liner, *Berengaria*, named after the daughter of Sanchez VI, King of Navarre, and Blanche of Castile, who was the Queen of Richard Cœur de Lion. There is assuredly good omen in the name chosen for the *Aquitania*, for does it not mean the "Land of the Waters", and was not "Aquitania" the richest of the three great divisions of Roman Gaul?

Preliminary designs of the liner were eventually drawn up by the company's staff of naval architects. The builders carried out a series of experiments, amongst the most important of which were those connected with the shape and design of the hull and the shape and sizes of the propellers. It need hardly be pointed out that, in order to attain as economically as possible the speed required, the inevitable resistance of the hull as it moves through the water must be reduced to a minimum and no expense must be spared in order to ascertain what is that minimum. The plan adopted by the builders of the *Aquitania* was the following: A wax model of the hull according to the preliminary design was made, and this model was attached to a movable carriage spanning a large experimental water tank some 400 feet in length and 20 feet in width and about 10 feet in depth. The model was drawn through the water at a rate proportionate to the designed speed of the ship, and intricate and delicate recording instruments noted the resistance of the water. By a series of such experiments it was possible to find the ideal shape to be given to the hull, and also the most suitable propellers. One of the most important modifications arrived at after the tank experiments in connection with the *Aquitania* had been carried out was the addition of about 15 feet to her length.

It might be mentioned in this connection that the data obtained at the time of the construction of the *Mauretania* some few years previously were of the greatest assistance. In the case of the latter ship her builders, Messrs. Swan, Hunter & Wigham-Richardson, of Newcastle, constructed a small launch with which they conducted experiments lasting over a period of two years. There were no fewer than 500 speed trials to determine the most suitable shape, size and position of the propellers; and 400 diagrams, each showing twelve tests, were prepared as a result.

It must be remembered that in the case of the *Aquitania* early in 1911, the builders were dealing with a ship of unprecedented weight, height, length and other abnormal features. In other words, they had never before had such an enormous ship to build. Therefore the situation demanded very careful consideration. For one thing, the whole face of their yard on the Clyde had to be changed. The same site or berth was used as that upon which the *Lusitania* was built, but owing to the much greater length of the *Aquitania* the preparation of the ground had to be considerably extended. It ran in line with the river Cart, which flows into the Clyde almost opposite the yard. This enabled the builders in launching the ship to avail themselves of the increased water area. The new ground was prepared in the same way as that for the *Lusitania*, but the part on which the earlier ship's structure had rested required, of course, comparatively little treatment beneath its surface.

In addition to the preparatory work in the shipyard itself, a good deal had to be done in the river with the object of ensuring enough room and sufficient depth of water for the liner when she was launched. A part of the river had to be widened opposite the yard for launching the *Lusitania*. Subsequently, in anticipating the launching of the *Aquitania* the widening was continued along the north side of Newshot Isle, i.e. along the south bank of the Clyde. The waterway between Clydebank and the tail of the bank off Greenock had to be dredged deeper in order that the ship could, without taking the slightest risk, make her way safely to the sea. Also the river immediately in front of the ship or berth had to be dredged, and special provision made to ensure that when the ship "dipped," on finally leaving the ways, there would be sufficient depth for her. Further dredging had also to be made to provide for a basin to accommodate the *Aquitania* when she was eventually waterborne, and to enable the final fitting-up to be done as she was lying in the river.

The design of the ship having been established in a form modified by experiments, the plans were ready to be worked out. A half-model was prepared in wood for the final approval of the lines of the ship. The operation of "drawing the lines" was then proceeded with, the contour of the vessel being transferred from the half-model to flat, marble-topped tables. In the meantime, calculators were busy determining from the plans how much material was required for the ship, and making out estimates for the cost of labour and so on.

The plans were then "laid out" in what is called the moulding loft. This is a vast, low-roofed structure, with a well-lighted expanse of smooth floor made dull black like a school blackboard. Here full-sized drawings of the different portions of the ship's skeleton were chalked out. From these chalk lines the curves were taken with wooden battens to serve as patterns for the actual framing of the ship. Other very important work was done here, such as the making and erecting of wooden pattern moulds for heavy plates. Finally the position of every rivet hole and the contours of every curve and twist were determined.

All the various workshops then started operations, and the company's furnishing department were studying the question of the furnishing of the ship. Orders for panelling, woodwork, bedsteads, carpets, chairs and a host of other similar articles were being placed. Steel from the furnaces was being prepared for rolling and forging into shape, and riveted and machined, so as to form a skeleton framing. Mild steel is used almost exclusively nowadays for building the hulls of ships. As you can well imagine, it would have been impossible to have built the *Aquitania* of wood. Mild steel can be forged and cast like iron, and is equally as strong in all directions. It also is very ductile, and can easily be drawn out into the required shape without cracking, whereas iron is brittle. Such scrupulous care is taken to ensure a safely constructed ship in these days that the metal used has to pass very serious tests to satisfy the Board of Trade and Lloyd's surveyors. Every inch of metal, too, has to be very carefully calculated, weight must be kept down as much as possible, and yet the strength of the hull must in no way be allowed to suffer.

In preparing the site two large berths in the east yard had to be converted into one big berth, and several buildings had to be pulled down. The liner needed a berth of over 300 yards in length. A new crane system had to be installed on either side to cope with the lifting of the heavy steel plates, girders and so on from the mass of accumulated material laying at her sides. The ground on which the ship was to be built had to be specially prepared. A steam roller was turned time and again over the surface. Immense piles were then driven in, and these were cross-piled. Over the cross piles were placed layers of heavy steel plates, then large quantities of cement were rolled smooth over the whole surface in order that there should be no movement of the foundations as the great ship grew and its weight increased. Along the entire length of the slipway, from the waterside inland, massive keel blocks were fitted. These keel blocks were composed of strong baulks of timber, piled one upon another at suitable distances apart along the keel line, and so adjusted that the keel laid upon a slight slope of about half an inch in every foot. This was to allow the ship to be easily and safely glided down to the water.

The keel was laid eventually in June, 1911. When one observes the size of this enormous vertical girder, lying flat and running along almost the entire length of the slipway, it is difficult to realise that such a solid mass of steel could ever form part of a body that floated on the water. In fact, this is the impression one gets of the whole structure as it is being assembled. Now the keel formed the centre of the foundations, and upon this the *Aquitania's* great vertebræ were gradually built up.

Day by day this great spine was added to by
the ribs of framing.  This delicate and difficult
job consisted of something more than joining
parts made to fit one another as one puts together
the pieces of a jig-saw puzzle.  With the aid of
almost human cranes capable of moving the heavy
castings and forgings to any required position,
the job certainly looked easy.  But each process
was the work of a group of specialised men who
had grown up with the work, and it was due to
their high efficiency and technical skill that the
difficult task was performed so smoothly and
rapidly.

The cranes employed consisted of seven derrick
cranes (which are a development of the old timber
derrick pole and gaff), and the ease with which
they could be moved greatly facilitated any rearrangement of the building berth.  Their maximum
load was five tons at an extreme radius of 55 ft.
and a minimum radius of 11 ft. 6 in.  The height
of the lift above the berth level was 111 ft. and the
total height of the mast 135 ft. overall.  Slewing
gear was provided to turn the jib through an
angle of over 200 degrees.  The power used was
electricity, and the motors were of the totally
enclosed reversing type.  The speeds of working
were hoisting, 5 tons at 60 ft. per minute, and
3 tons at 100 ft. per minute; racking, 5 tons at

35 ft. per minute; and slewing, 5 tons at 200 degrees per minute.

Armies of workmen were now busying themselves at the bottom of the ship and working up into position the side framing, first amidships and then gradually extending in either direction towards the stem and to the stern, until eventually the ship presented the appearance of the skeleton of an enormous animal lying on its back. The work of putting on the flesh and the skin crept on, and a few weeks later the ship took more shape. The thickness of the shell-plating of the skin amidships throughout from the keel to the bridge deck was just over an inch, all riveted together by hydraulic riveters. Before the plating was proceeded with, of course, the enormous beams which span the inside had to be put into place to take the decks. Now the *Aquitania* has in all nine decks—named the boat deck, promenade deck, bridge deck, shelter deck, upper deck, main deck, lower deck, orlop deck, and lower orlop deck. The last named, however, is only partial, extending forward and abaft the machinery space only. The main structure of the ship finishes at the bridge deck, which extends for some 525 ft. amidships as a structural deck, and is continued 115 ft. abaft this length as a superstructure deck of lighter scantling.

The boat deck has a length of 453 ft. over the midships portion of the ship, with a further 50 ft. over the after deckhouses. The promenade deck extends for a length of 624 ft. The boat and promenade decks have no camber to them, and extend over the hull, as it were, about 2 ft. in order to give more space for promenading and more room for handling the boats.

To finish off, the framing of the ship, a most intricate operation, had to be faced. That involved the erection of the massive stem and stern frames, made of solid cast steel. The total finished weight of the stern frame and the brackets which take the great propeller shaft was 130 tons, whilst the cast steel rudder weighed no less than 70 tons, the extreme width of the blade measuring 28 ft., and the stock of forged steel having a diameter of no less than $18\frac{1}{2}$ inches. It is interesting to note that over seventy-five tons of molten metal were used in casting the main pieces of the stern frame. Owing to its immense size, it had to be conveyed from the forge at Darlington to the yard at Clydebank on a Sunday, as the load overhung the tracks to such an extent that the whole railway *en route* had to be kept clear of traffic, and a Sunday was the only day on which this job could be carried out satisfactorily.

In order to enlarge our acquaintance with the ship as far as completed let us descend into the depths. After traversing the whole of the nine decks, we find ourselves standing on what are called the tank tops, below which is the double bottom. This double bottom is well over six feet in depth under the engine room. It is sub-divided into forty-one compartments and the hull itself is divided into eighty-four water-tight compartments.

Quite an accurate impression of the ship can be gained by thinking of her as an immense steel box. Below the bottom of this box must be added a false bottom, which is divided, into forty-one compartments. The box itself is divided up longitudinally by tall, steel bulk-heads, and that space again divided by other bulkheads running at right angles. In the box itself, and the false bottom, there are no fewer than 125 separate boxes, all watertight compartments. At a distance from the sides corre-sponding to 18 ft. in the ship herself, there is an inner skin separated by steel bulkheads from the outer skin.

This sub-dividing is carried out in such a way as to render her actually a ship within a ship. The arrangement serves a double purpose of carrying water and of ensuring additional safety in the event of the ship being holed. For if by collision, or striking a rock the outer skin became fractured, and water flowed in, this flooding could be limited to a small area by closing the watertight doors in the compartments affected. In addition there are sixteen bulkheads extending athwartship from the port to the starboard side.

Next we come to the screw propellers. The screw propeller of any ship should be second to no other item of the ship in importance. It is remarkable how comparatively little change there has been in the design of the screw propeller since its superiority over the old paddle wheel for ocean-going vessels was demonstrated about seventy years ago. In the early days of screw propellers there were, of course, many freak designs, but now a type has been developed which is almost stereotyped. The fixing of the dimensions of a screw propeller is one of those problems to the solution of which there is no royal road.

The *Aquitania* has four screw propellers, each of which is four bladed, the blades and boss being cut solid in high-tension manganese bronze. In view of the great size of the ship, it might well be asked, why four? The number of screws depends upon various considerations. By far the largest number of ships are fitted with single screws. Nearly all passenger ships, and many warships, have twin screws, while many of the higher powered ships have three, and in the case of large express liners such as the *Aquitania* four are fitted. The advent of the different types of propelling machinery has brought varying factors into the problem. Thus the reciprocating steam engine followed a normal development, one or two screws being adopted mainly as dictated by the requirements of the ship. When the steam turbine became practicable a new set of conditions had to be faced, with the result that multiple screws became common, three and four shafts becoming the rule, rather than the exception, while in some ships two screws were fitted on each shaft, one behind the other, as far apart as possible. Combination machinery of reciprocating engines and turbines resulted, inevitably, in three and four screws being adopted.

The adoption of geared turbines has brought things back to a more normal condition, and single and twin screws are now fitted as required by purely ship conditions. The introduction of oil engines has tended to create a preference for the use of twin rather than single screws for reasons dependent largely on the limitations of this type of engine.

From the ship point of view, the size of the ship, apart from the power of the propelling machinery, is a deciding factor, in many cases, between single and twin screws. Two screws are always safer than one, and if the size or value of the ship justifies it twin screws are always to be preferred to single screws. The navigation of the ship is also an important consideration. A single screw ship without "way on" is a helpless thing. A twin screw ship is more manageable, and in special cases, therefore, where difficulties in navigation are important, two screws are to be preferred.

From the point of view of efficiency in propulsion, considerable importance attaches to the choice of number of screws. Where the ship's draught is adequate, thus putting no great limit upon propeller diameter, and where the type of machinery does not limit the revolutions, there is no question that the single screw should be the most efficient. Under similar conditions twin screws will be slightly better than triple screws, and triple screws better than four screws. Usually, however, limitations do exist, and then it becomes a matter of choosing what is the best course to follow. The least number of screws is the best generally speaking, but large power calls for either a large propeller or for two or more propellers. If the former cannot be given, the latter will be necessary. Duplication of screws however, adds to the weight of machinery required, but some compensation is obtained from the fact that higher revolutions may reasonably be adopted as the number of screws is increased. That is the main reason why four screws were considered essential for a ship of enormous size and power like the *Aquitania*.

# CHAPTER II

THE riveting to the frames of all plates forming
the skin was now completed and the outside surface of the hull up to the load water-line was
given its conventional coating of salmon-pink
composition, whilst the lower portion of the hull
was painted black. Meanwhile, the bossing for the
shafts, then the shafts themselves, together with
the propellers and also the rudder, were then set
up in their positions. The next step, and one of
the most critical and difficult, was to transfer the
ship from the land and safely let her slide into the
water. It might be said that no moment in the
life of a ship is quite so important as her christening and launch, and it is right and proper that it
should be the occasion for entertainment and
general rejoicings, as is nearly always the case.
In these days, it is the usual thing for a lady to be
asked to stand sponsor for the new vessel, but this
is quite a comparatively modern idea, which came

into use in this country by the wish of one of the early Georges. Before that time the entire ceremony was carried out by men.

But the launching of a great ship is much more than a mere spectacular episode in its career. The problem of a launch, reduced to its elements, is to shift a weight of some thousands of tons down to the water over a length of several hundred feet by means of innumerable pieces of wood and some hundredweights of soft soap and tallow. The hull has been resting on its keel blocks and four rows of shores or supports on each side. First comes the stupendous task of transferring the weight of the ship from the keel blocks underneath to the "cradles" resting on the ways, or long paths or platforms, leading down to the river. There is one launchway on the port side and one on the starboard side. Each side consists of a set of "groundways" or "standing ways" fixed to and remaining on the berth, and a set of "sliding ways" which, though not actually attached to the ship, hold her in a kind of cradle in such a way that they remain under her till she is water-borne. The standing ways are laid at a steeper slope than that upon which the ship has been built. On top of these are the sliding ways, and in the space between them and the ship's bottom, a series of packing logs is inserted.

The first process of the operations is to transfer the weight of the ship from the building support blocks to the launching ways. This is done by placing a continuous layer of wedges on both sides of each sliding way, where they are driven up by a long line of shipwrights all driving them at the same time. The process is known as "setting-up," and is carried out some hours before the actual time of the launch. The next step is to apply lubricant, usually consisting of tallow and soft soap, to the touching surfaces of both sets of ways. In very hot or very cold weather special precautions have to be taken to ensure the grease being kept in good condition, for, as you can imagine, either the melting or the freezing of the lubricants might have serious consequences.

On the day of the launch, careful consideration having been given to the state of the tide, the keel and bilge blocks underneath the ship are slightly slacked and reduced in number. This process goes on steadily during the day, leaving as much support as possible to save weight on the grease, but steadily working down to a number which can be removed during the last half-hour prior to the actual launch. Meanwhile the most careful observations are being maintained of the "liveliness" of the ship, that is to say, its increasing tendency to move as the successive supports are withdrawn. The final stage before the actual launch is to release the remainder of the keel and bilge blocks so that the ship is merely kept poised in position for the launch by the mechanical triggers or steel clamps attached to the launching ways, the release of which will leave the ship free to start moving down the ways stern first. It cannot safely be kept hanging in that position for long, and the creaking of timber and the draw on the gauges issue a continual warning.

Once the vessel has been started on its eventful journey down the ways, the next problem is to stop it soon after it reaches the water This is often a serious matter, as many shipyards have very restricted river space. The checking is usually accomplished by means of wire ropes or cables leading from the hull to progressively acting drag weights or buried anchors up each side of the berth. This problem is of special importance in the case of a ship of the size of the *Aquitania*, as we shall see later on.

We have now described, as briefly as possible, the various stages necessary to transfer the enormous weight of a big ship from the ways to the water. Let us now examine the special arrangements for the launch of the *Aquitania* in more detail.

Reference has already been made briefly to the many preparations, in anticipation of the launch, that had to be made before the keel was laid.

The technical staff attached to the shipyard had, in the meanwhile, carefully calculated the dimensions, the slope and camber required on the launching ways to carry the ship into the water. These calculations were governed by the size and weight of the ship, and the speed she would make when she started to move.

To shift a mighty mass of so many thousand tons was a task of no mean order. The slightest hitch might mean fatal injury to the hull, upon which so much thought, time and money had been spent.

The launching ways, as has been already stated, were constructed of pitch pine, oak being used at the forward end of the sliding ways to take the extra pressure when the ship began to lift after entering the water. Launching ways, generally, are designed to take an average pressure per square foot of about two tons, increasing to about eight tons at the aft end of the ways when the stern of the vessel begins to float.

In April, 1913, when the *Aquitania* was advanced to the stage when final preparations for launching had to begin, the standing ways were placed in position extending from the forward end of the ship to the water edge at low tide. The foundation was made up of longitudinal wood logs and transverse blocks, all of pitch pine. The ways were placed on top and secured in place by side shores, angle stays and brackets to counteract any outward and longitudinal thrust. The sliding ways, extending from the forward end of the ship to the stern, were then placed in position on top of the standing ways. On the inside edge of the sliding ways was fixed a rubbing piece of elm overlapping the standing ways by about three inches. This formed a guide, and also counteracted any tendency of the sliding ways to spread under the pressure of the ship's weight on its way down to the water. The space between the top of the sliding ways and the shell plating was made up with wood packing, a space being left for the insertion of two hardwood wedges.

At the ends, where the ship is "V" shaped, other arrangements had to be made to bridge the space between the ways and the ship. As is the usual practice, a temporary steel structure was attached to the hull, projecting far enough to overhang the ways and to afford a flat bearing surface to the wood packing. Heavy wood logs were then fitted between the sliding ways and the underside of the temporary structure on the hull. A sufficient space was left between the wood logs and the ways to allow of soft wood packing and two hardwood wedges being inserted. The wood logs referred to are called "poppets", and the whole structure at the bow and stern is usually known as the ship's cradle. The structure at the bow had to be made very strong, as a considerable load was thrown on the fore poppets when the stern began to float. After the structure forming the cradles and the wood packing and wedges for the whole length of the ship were fitted in place, it was marked, numbered and removed. The sliding ways were lifted clear of the standing ways, and the bearing surface of both ways coated with a mixture of hot tallow and oil applied with a brush so as to minimise friction, and to ensure a smooth and ready movement. After the tallow had cooled an application of black soft soap in blobs about six inches apart was put on top of the tallow and oil. The sliding ways were then replaced and also all the packing, wedges and cradles already mentioned, the wedges being slightly driven in to keep the material in place.

Arrangements were then made for holding the ship in place when all the wood blocks under the keel, bilge blocks, and shores were removed, which was done a short while before the ship was actually launched. Large hardwood rams, with their ends iron bound, and hand grips on each side, were suspended from the deck. Each ram was manned by a number of workmen, and all the wedges already referred to in connection with the making up of the ways and cradles were rammed so that the weight of the ship was taken up by the launching ways. All other supports, such as keel blocks, bilge blocks, and the remainder of the shores were removed, and the ship was ready to move. The actual ceremony took place at high tide, when there was sufficient height of water on the end of the ways to avoid any danger to the ship.

A hydraulic power system was employed to release the great hull of the *Aquitania*, and thus to send it gliding down the ways. This controlled all the arrangements for holding the ship after the supports had been removed and the weight taken up by the launching ways. A hydraulic cylinder was placed at the bow, and connected to a number of triggers made of steel arranged at intervals on each side of the ship and attached to the launching ways. The triggers

A Striking Bow View of the "Aquitania" on The Stocks

FLAG SIGNALS ON BIDSTON HILL

THIS CONTEMPORARY SKETCH SHOWS THE METHOD ADOPTED FOR CONVEYING NEWS OF
VESSELS APPROACHING THE MERSEY SOME FIFTY YEARS BEFORE THE FIRST CUNARDER
SAILED FROM THE PORT. "EACH MERCHANT OF IMPORTANCE HAD HIS OWN SIGNAL, AND
THE MOMENT THE LOOKOUT MAN AT BIDSTON COULD IDENTIFY A SHIP APPROACHING THE
RIVER HE WOULD RUN UP THE FLAG OF THE TRADER CONCERNED. IN THIS WAY THE NEWS
OF AN INCOMING VESSEL PRECEDED ITS ARRIVAL BY SEVERAL HOURS."

DRESSING THE WAX MODEL

THE EXPERIMENTAL TANK

were held in place by a clip controlled by the
hydraulic system, and a connection was taken from
the cylinder to a table on the launching platform
and controlled by a button which was pressed
by the Countess of Derby, who was the honoured
lady on this occasion. The action of pressing the
button released the clip holding the triggers in
position, and left the ship free to glide down the
ways. The electric gear working thus operated
simultaneously with the mechanism for throwing
the christening bottle against the side of the
ship. When the triggers were released there
was no perceptible movement for quite three
minutes, but there was evidence, in the creaking
noise, that the laws of gravity were steadily
asserting themselves. Then, after fully three
minutes' creaking, for reasons which we have
already explained, the mighty mass began to
move, and from the first indication of perceptible motion until she was afloat one minute
thirty-one seconds elapsed, which gives an
average speed, as we have said, of about 10 ft.
per second.

To check the vessel, in view of the limited space
in the river, there were eight piles of chains on
each side of the berth, and these were connected
by wire ropes secured to very heavy eye-bolts
riveted temporarily to the sides of the ship. The

collective weight of these chain-drags was just under 1,400 tons, and the aftermost drag came into effect just before the bow of the ship had left the ways. Thus the brake was very gentle and gradual in its application. That it was effective is proved by the fact that the vessel was pulled up when only about 150 ft. from the end of the ways, and that two of the piles of drags on each side were never moved. The total time taken from the release of the triggers until the vessel dipped from the end of the ways was five minutes ten seconds. The draught forward was found to be 13 ft., and aft 21 ft., the launching weight, without the ways or cradle, being about 22,000 tons.

In view of the special arrangements that had been made because of the extraordinary size of the ship, and the preparations, on an abnormally extensive scale, which had been carried out on shore, it will be readily appreciated that it was with a tremendous sigh of relief that the vast crowd of people gathered to witness the ceremony, and more especially those who were responsible for her creation, saw her at last riding the waters of the Clyde.

But her liberty was quite short-lived, as seven powerful tugs got hold of her and led her carefully into the neighbouring basin to receive her engines

and much else besides, including the most artistic
and costly luxuries that money could buy,
which have rendered her famous the world over.
Flags now fluttered down from the long, wide
berth which she had just vacated; the thousands
of spectators who had witnessed this historic
ceremony left the scene; the last strip of bunting
and flags were put away; the high tide ebbed out.
To the joy of every one, and the relief of all those
who were responsible for her conception and
launching, this huge, beautiful liner with the lines
of a yacht and bows as fine as a fast torpedo boat,
was at last brought to rest, safely moored alongside
the special fitting-out quay, within an hour of her
launch.

Mr. E. Keble Chatterton, who was amongst
the guests at the ceremony, writing an impression
just prior to the launch, said: "I have watched
the growth of the *Aquitania* from that mass of
inanimate metal to a towering steel structure of
singular strength and exquisite design. I have
been privileged to see storey after storey rise upon
their strong foundations. I have walked in and
out along the numerous decks, I have lost myself
in the maze of girders, regarded with marvel
and amazement the long avenues of steel converg-
ing in the dim distance, just as, when standing
at a wayside station, you see the railway track

" vanishing into space a long way off. I asked myself whether it was true that I was standing on a ship, whether it was not an enormous town hall or some new Houses of Parliament that they were building firmly to the ground. There was the width of the broadest highway on her deck with ample room for footpaths and the busiest vehicular traffic to pass and repass. I climbed higher still to the next deck, and the first obvious suggestion was that this vast space would be ample for two first-class football teams to decide a cup tie. And then I reminded myself, and had to keep on remembering, that the whole of this amazing structure was only temporarily sojourning on land, that it was being built to float on water, that, excepting for the rare occasions when the hull needed attention in dry dock, the *Aquitania* would never again rest her weight on mother earth.

"It seemed like a page from Gulliver. Here and there ran railway lines up and down the ship. Those tiny black dots busying themselves near the stern were found presently to be a gang of stalwart riveters. Could it be possible that all this steel building would ever be moved half an inch nearer the water, let alone launched safely?"

Although she had come to life, she was yet far

from being complete. Over a year of unceasing activity was necessary before the ship would be ready for service. During the whole of this period hundreds of men were at work on the sides and in the interior. Some were hydraulic riveting, others trimming the steel structure with hydraulic chisels, others cutting out great slabs of solid steel. Down in the depths of the vessel still more were busy preparing for the reception of the turbines and shafts. At the lowest point, workmen were painting the inside of the double bottom; on the decks above, partitions were being erected which in due course would develop into public rooms and state-rooms. Miles of electric wires were being laid along seemingly endless corridors, plasterers were fixing ceilings; numerous solid staircases were being built from the lowest to the highest decks. From all parts of the country truckloads of all kinds of manufactured articles were arriving, and month after month thousands of skilled men were working in order to make the ship what a great art critic described as "the ship beautiful." Through the spaces left in the decks the boilers and turbines were swung in and lowered by a big 150-ton crane, and the four great funnels, each large enough to permit of a railway loco-motive passing through it, were hoisted on board and set up.

Completed with all her machinery and with her passenger accommodation almost finished, she left the Clydebank works on May 10th, 1914, to make her way to the sea. There was little need of anxiety, notwithstanding her great length and the narrowness of the channel through which she had to pass. The engineer-in-chief of the Clyde Trust had worked assiduously during the building of the ship to satisfy himself, by soundings and other means, that all that could be done had been accomplished for the passage of the ship. All that was now necessary was a calm day. This was realised, and if the drizzling rain that fell was a discomfort to the five hundred thousand to six hundred thousand people gathered along the banks of the river, the breeze added a touch of the mysterious to the slow but continuously steady progress of the majestic ship with her attendant tugs, preceded by the Clyde Trust commodore steamer, and a convoy of pleasure steamers. She came out of the mist in her great bulk, passed by the crowds gathered at each vantage point, and receded again in impressive, stately silence. When she eventually reached the Firth, however, the weather cleared and the sun shone. She then made a short spin at 8 or 9 knots, twelve boilers being alight. Finally, she anchored to coal up and prepare for her trials.

These trials are essentially an occasion for the demonstration by the shipbuilder that the organs which give the ship life are running efficiently.

It was decided that the trials should be of short duration, especially as this afforded a greater period of time for the final preparation of the ship to take up her station on the 30th May. As regards the attainment of the guaranteed speed, this had become almost a matter of precision, in view of the possibility of determining from models the power necessary to drive at a given rate of speed a ship of certain lines, and with the best propulsive efficiency. The proportions and lines of the *Aquitania* were determined by the model tests carried out at the experimental tank at Clydebank already mentioned, so that there was little doubt about the realisation of the speed on the trials or in service.

On May 11th the vessel took on board over 2,000 tons of coal and water ballast to bring her down to the mean draught she would reach while on the Atlantic voyage. On the following day she left her anchorage for her trials, with the intention not so much of ascertaining her speed for the designed full power, as to test the turbines and their manœuvring gear, to ensure that all auxiliaries were in thoroughly satisfactory order, and also to get the engine-room staff fully acquainted with their duties. The turbines were therefore worked up gradually to full power, and opportunity was taken to make runs over the measured mile at Skelmorlie at progressive speeds, beginning at 12 knots.

As far as the "measured mile" trials were concerned, the procedure was as follows: The telegraph bell in the engine-room gave three rings—a sign from the bridge that the ship would be at the "measured mile" in about three minutes. Another ring, and the "measured mile" was commenced, and the time noted to the fifth part of a second. When the mile had been covered, the telegraph bell rang again, and the time was once more carefully noted.

All the data could not, however, be regarded as accurately determining the relation of power to speed, as the vessel had been in the tidal basin since her launch thirteen months ago, so that the immersed part of the hull was dirty and in a condition which involved excessive skin resistance. On Tuesday afternoon the vessel proceeded into the outer estuary of the Clyde, where a greater seaway was available for manœuvring purposes, and the engineer had greater freedom for testing the valves when changing over from triple series

working to compound working, and for bringing
the turbines on the port and starboard side
of the ship into action for ahead and astern
steaming.   It was important to take note of how
much time was occupied in changing over from
full speed ahead to full speed astern.   Steering
trials to test the power and sensitiveness of the
steering gear and the response of the ship to
the helm, and further trials of the telegraph,
windlass, steam whistle, watertight doors, and
the special type of auxiliary machinery had to be
undergone.

Following upon this a series of high-power and
full-power runs were made between Holy Isle and
Ailsa Craig.   The wind had steadily increased,
but, notwithstanding the unsatisfactory state of
the immersed hull, the result was satisfactory,
speeds of 24 knots being reached without any
effort; there was accordingly every confidence of
the guaranteed speed of 23 knots on the Atlantic
being exceeded.   The night was spent at sea,
running under various conditions of working, but
principally for introducing the engineers of the
ship to their work.   On the Wednesday again
there were further full-power runs, equally satisfactory.   Instruments were carried, and other
methods adopted to register any possibility of
vibration, but in no case was any such move-

ment indicated. This demonstrates the success of the special care taken in the direction of stiffening the ship, a matter already referred to in connection with the building of the structure of the ship.

# CHAPTER III

## MACHINERY AND ENGINEERS

IT might be asked what is it exactly that excites the wonder and glamour which surrounds a modern liner? Is it the steel hull? Wonderful steel bridges and towers and other similar structures might challenge any claim that a ship may have in this direction. Is it the internal arrangements, the public rooms, and their gorgeous decorations, swimming baths, gymnasia? Modern hotels can show equal, and in some cases superior, arrangements of this sort. Is it not the fact that a ship is in a sense alive, which, as Ruskin wrote, "makes it the most honourable thing that man has ever produced." That an enormous floating hotel as long as the Houses of Parliament and broader than the Strand in London, weighing about fifty thousand tons, can be moved from Southampton to New York within a week, turned round, stopped or set into motion again at will, is without doubt a marvel. What is it that gives it this life? The machinery? The machines that drive her, and give her power, have often been referred to as the heart of the ship, but no sooner is this simile applied than someone has retorted, yes! and the bridge is the brains or the eye, to which the electrician has switched in with the remark that his cables are the nerves, and the plumber his pipes as the veins and arteries. But it is hardly necessary to state that the nerves, veins and brains can be deranged, and yet the heart will continue to function, which points to the machinery being the most important organ in the whole ship's system, says the chief engineer.

Within the limit of a chapter it is, of course, impossible to give anything like an adequate idea of so extensive and so technical a subject as the *Aquitania's* turbines. Altogether they weigh some nine thousand tons and occupy about 84 ft. of the ship's length. Their designed power at 165 revolutions is some sixty thousand horse-power for an ocean speed of twenty-three knots. To describe the whole marvellous mechanism would mean to involve you, perhaps, in a maze of bewildering and boring technicalities.

For those who do not understand the principle of the working of a turbine, it may be helpful for a moment to forget about the ship entirely, and to think of some little village by the countryside where there is a working watermill. It will be seen that the water revolves the wheel by its pressure against the series of blades on which it falls. The shaft, which goes through the centre of the wheel, is connected with the machinery which it actuates. Apply the motion to the steam turbine, consisting of an enormous steel drum, or casing, weighing about 140 tons, through which passes a shaft or spindle fixed to a series of wheels on the rims of which are not merely a few blades but hundreds of thousands. The steam, when admitted at one end of the casing, rushes through to the other end, and its passage is so deflected as to exert pressure against the blades, which, carrying the wheels with them, set up a rotating motion, and thus turn also the shaft or spindle, at the other end of which is the screw propeller.

This is roughly the principle of a Parsons turbine, with which the ship is fitted. The power is generated, of course, in the following manner. The heat of the furnaces, which, by the way, have a total heating surface of nearly 140,000 square feet, acting on the water in her twenty-one double-ended cylindric boilers, turns it into steam. The steam is carried by large pipes into the engine-room.

The turbines are arranged in what is known as treble series, so that the steam passes through the high-pressure turbine on the port wing shaft, exhausting into the intermediate-pressure turbine on the starboard wing shaft, which in turn passes its steam to two low-pressure turbines, one on each of the two inner shafts.

It must be remembered that a turbine can only run one way, so for driving astern there are turbines on all four shafts.  On the port shaft is a high-pressure turbine separate from the ahead turbine, and exhausting into a low-pressure astern turbine on the port inner shaft.  This low-pressure astern turbine is incorporated in the same casing as the low-ahead turbine; while on the starboard outer shaft there is also a separate high-pressure turbine, exhausting in a low-pressure astern turbine on the starboard inner shaft.

The adoption of the treble-series system for ahead working has required a considerable amount of ingenuity to ensure that the turbines can be worked independently of any one which may be thrown out of action; and it may be said here that even with one turbine thrown out of gear there is little or no difficulty in maintaining sufficient power to reach full speed.

The steam pressure diminishes after the steam presses through each turbine, until it finally goes

to the condensers. A condenser is really a sort
of gigantic still, in which the steam comes into
contact with some 18,700 small pipes, through
which are pumped every hour about 18,500 tons
of cold sea water. By contact with these pipes
the steam is condensed. Some of you, looking
at a big steamer, will have seen a stream of
water pouring out of a big hole or pipe in
the hull of the ship. This is the water being
discharged from the condenser after it has done
its work.

The chief engineer of the *Aquitania* would
probably tell you that his department of the ship,
especially to the office people ashore, is a sort of
"fly in the ointment," a "thorn in the flesh".
Why? First, because it is a non-producer,
and does not show a profit in the company's
books. Secondly, it is the most costly and
expensive department in the ship to operate.
Thirdly, it is apt to get deranged and cause dis-
location, and therefore run the ship and the company into untold expenses. For when a breakdown
occurs, or a passenger complains that his room is
too hot, or his bath-water is too cold, or the ventilation of his cabin is not good, or perishable
cargo does not turn out correct—with all these
affairs, the engineers are associated. But it should
be remembered that the engineers' department in

the ship is practically the only one where anything can go wrong.

The space below "F" deck is for the greater part of the ship's length devoted to the main and auxiliary engines, boilers and fuel bunkers. Owing to the exceptional length of the vessel it was found desirable to introduce compartments between the boiler rooms, running crosswise, mainly in order to secure a suitable spacing for the four huge funnels. The boilers were arranged three abreast in central compartments about sixty feet wide, of which the fore and aft sides are formed by continuous watertight divisions placed some eighteen feet from the outer skin of the ship, the intervening spaces being used for carrying fuel.

As already stated, in dealing with the construction of the hull, these divisions or bulkheads constitute an inner skin, which adds greatly to the safety of the vessel in case of damage to the outer shell. There are four boiler rooms altogether, the three foremost ones each containing six boilers, while that nearest the engine room contains three boilers.

When the *Aquitania* was originally placed in service, a month or two before the outbreak of the war, she was fitted as a coal burner. Some 900 tons of coal was her daily consumption.

During the war she played many parts in Government service and happily survived them all. After being returned to her normal service in 1919 the Cunard company, in view of the fact that considerable work was necessary to put the ship back into the rôle of a peaceful trader, decided that the time was opportune to consider converting her from a coal- to an oil-burner. This work was entrusted to Armstrong, Whitworth & Co., on the Tyne, and very successfully they carried it out. Provision was made for the carriage of over 9,000 tons of oil, which is practically sufficient to take the ship across the Atlantic and back. The change has been an unqualified success.

There are scientists who criticise shipowners for being so wasteful as to burn oil in this way under boilers, and say that the proper method of using oil is in an explosive or Diesel engine. Probably they are right. Engineers and metallurgists are still persevering in this direction, and for comparatively moderate power have met with a great deal of success. But it is thought in many quarters the time is not yet ripe for applying these engines to ships of the *Aquitania* type, where effective horse-power of anything from 60,000 to 80,000 is required to drive them at their working speed.

The following figures will give an idea of the immensity of the work carried out in converting her to an oil-fuel burner. It meant the removal from the boiler rooms of 300 tons of material; and 650 tons of new material were introduced. No fewer than 95 tons of rivets were used, while 11,300 yards of steel piping were required. At the commencement of this enormous work over 800 men were put on board, and this number increased, week by week, until there was a total of 2,500 men employed each week. In addition, several hundred women were employed, making a total of about 3,000.

One of the advantages claimed by the use of oil fuel is the additional cargo space available, due to the fuel being carried in the ship's cellular double-bottom tanks. The *Aquitania* not being a large cargo carrier, it was not a practicable proposition to utilise the original coal bunkers for cargo purposes. As no great advantage was to be gained by using the double-bottom tanks for storing the oil, it was decided to reconstruct the coal bunkers for that purpose. In this space, extending the full length of the boiler space, a matter of 370 ft., the oil is carried. In addition to these side bunkers, large athwart-ship bunkers have also been made suitable for oil carrying.

On each side of the ship there are four connections for fuelling purposes. Should all the connections on one side of the ship be in use at one time, it would be possible to fuel the vessel completely in about six hours. Special precautions have been taken to avoid against over-filling of tanks. An overflow storage tank is provided in each group of tanks in each boiler room, port and starboard. Each storage tank is provided with what is called a "pneumercator gauge," by means of which the depth of oil in the tanks can be noted at any time. From the storage tanks the oil is pumped by large vertical pumps to the settling tanks in duplicate. Two of these transfer pumps are fitted in each boiler room. The capacity of each settling tank is such as to ensure sixteen hours' supply for three double-ended boilers, so that about fifteen hours will be allowed for the settling of the oil in one tank while the other tank is in use. From the settling tanks the oil pressure pumps take their supply through suction strainers, discharging through the heaters and discharge filters to the burners in the furnaces.

It is quite possible that you will ask why the owners committed themselves to such enormous expenditure when the *Aquitania's* steaming powers from coal burning were so satisfactory. Oil burning has several advantages which justify such a huge outlay. As is well-known, with coal-fired boilers there is always a considerable loss of steam every watch, through burning down and cleaning of fires. In the *Aquitania* there are 168 furnaces. Assuming that twenty-eight fires are cleaned every watch, approximately 8,000 horse-power is lost every four hours. With oil-fired boilers there is no such loss incurred, as the oil can be supplied continuously to the burners and the heating maintained so that a constant steam pressure can be kept up. This has the effect of improving the speed of the vessel.

Then there is the absence of noise and dust, too, when bunkering, which must not be overlooked in a vessel of this type and size.

From the point of view of the working conditions of the crew, the changes which have been made as a result of this conversion are very considerable. An inspection below decks, as the ship gets up steam for sailing day, reveals in the boiler room a miniature army of men, cleanly clad, many of them in spotless white overalls. The boiler-house itself is as clean as a housewife's kitchen, and with a temperature as comfortable as that in the dining saloons above. Contrast this with the time when the same vessel used to operate with coal under her boilers. No fewer

than 168 hungry furnaces had to be fed to move
this great structure, and a staff of grim workers
numbering 350 were at work in shifts day and
night. Trimmers, passers and firemen, stripped
to the waist, with a piece of wet cloth round their
necks, laboured to move the thousands of tons of
coal from the bunkers of the ship into the in-
satiable mouths of the furnaces.

Life in the ship is totally different to-day. The
number of men below decks is but little more
than one-third what it was in the days of coal-
firing, and the call for increased steam is met
with the turn of a wrist and a valve. Gone are
the days of the grimy crew at the furnaces; gone,
too, are the long waits at Southampton and New
York, while hundreds of coal passers laboured
transferring thousands of tons of coal from barge
to bunkers. Now the crew, except for a skeleton
force on duty, are through with their work when
the vessel docks. Almost before the passengers
are off with their baggage, an oil tank vessel
carrying upwards of 7,000 tons of oil draws alongside, a hose is swung into position, and the
necessary connections are made.

As in most other professions or trades, com-
petition has effected a general speeding-up. A
modern ship costs so much to build and also so
much to run, that her owners cannot afford to

keep her idle for a day longer than is absolutely necessary, and so more effective methods and machinery are continually being brought into use.

When it is realised that a modern giant ship is worth probably over £3,000,000, and that the interest on this great amount at a low rate, even for one day, is not a negligible item, it will be seen that in order to pay for herself the ship must be earning money continually. One day's delay in port involves not only wages for the crew, but also dock and harbour charges. The necessity for a quick turnround in port is further accentuated by the immense increase in running cost that has taken place since the war. In consequence, the sailor, whether he be seaman, engineer, purser or steward, may well make up his mind that his home is in actual fact on the sea. The strenuousness of the life tends to increase still more year by year, but at the same time it is pleasant to know that the candidates for a seafaring career are as plentiful as ever.

## The Engineers

All have probably read of the engineers in swagger uniform, with gold lace, operating shining steel levers, and may have imagined that they have a very easy time at their job. But have they ever pictured the same engineers down in the bilges, waist-deep in cold, slimy liquid, removing an obstruction from some pipe or other, and imagined them afterwards endeavouring to remove some of the filth with a bucket of paraffin and a sponge? Somewhere between these two extremes, perhaps, lies the truth of the engineer's normal duties. It has already been seen how the continual running of the engines for days on end necessitates the closest attention on the part of the engineer on watch, but in addition he has to maintain a proper level of water in the boilers; otherwise there may be a serious accident. He must see that all furnaces are properly attended to; otherwise reduction in speed will ensue. He has also to keep very important records. Any little breakages that occur have, of course, to be remedied at once—there is quite a big workshop on board for this. In handing over his watch to his relieving colleague he has to satisfy him that everything is working satisfactorily; otherwise he must remain on watch until things have been rectified. At least once a year, in dry dock, propellers, sea-water valves and under-sea connections have to be inspected.

In a giant ship of the *Aquitania* type the qualifications of both officers and staff must be of the highest, and it is characteristic of the line to which they belong that the traditions and record have produced a sense of loyalty and *esprit de corps* for which a parallel can hardly be found. As far as the engineers are concerned, they are expected to qualify themselves with the highest certificates obtainable at as early a date as possible. Consequently, every ship contains a large number of men, even amongst the junior ratings, fully qualified to act as chief engineers.

In the first chapter reference was made to the experiments carried out with models in a large tank, which helped to arrive at the total resistance or power required to push or tow the ship through the water at the desired speed. It will be remembered also that a good deal of important data was obtained by a series of progressive power and speed runs over a measured mile at the time of the ship's trials before she was actually handed over by her builders. At this time, of course, she was not down to her loaded draught, having no cargo or other weighty materials aboard. In due course when she came into the service the economy of the ship was then definitely proved. Each day throughout the voyage the engineers keep a careful log, which records scientifically, among other things, the

speed and fuel consumption; and when she has
been sailing a few months, sufficient data are
available to show fuel consumption, power and
speed.   It will reveal, perhaps, that it is not economical to run the ship above or below a certain
speed; it may also show that she varies slightly
from the speed for which she was originally
designed,

All these data prove very useful when a new
ship is being built.   It may not be without interest
here to show how from the very earliest days
of the Cunard Line this collecting of data has
been made a very special point.

A perusal of the instructions issued to
Captain Woodruff, of the *Britannia*, the first
Cunarder, before she sailed on her first voyage, in
1840, shows the anxiety felt regarding the fuel
consumption.   The following extract covers this
point:

"You should make it the duty of the Officer
on Deck to ask the Engineers at regular intervals
if they have blown off the Boiler, and count
the revolutions of the Engines every two hours,
putting them down in the Log. You have on
board the *Britannia* ........ Tons coals. Would
recommend you not to work expansively for
first three days.

"The vessel being deepish at starting, fire *light*
—give her the full benefit of the steam pressure,

keeping just to the verge of blowing off steam, but none allowed to escape.

"Your consumption of coal will be light if the Furnace Doors are kept as much shut as possible, and a judicious use made of the Damper.

"As she lightens, work her expansively—if you have smart leading wind, 2nd or 3rd Grade should carry her along fast. If head wind, or heavy impeding sea, perhaps you should keep to the first Grade.

"When you are half passage, if you find you have about 400 tons Coals still left, get over the next half of the passage at the first Cut off, or full pressure without cutting off, as you deem most beneficial. It is very desirable in this instance to make a quick run to Halifax and Boston, but it will not do to work all this half of the passage at full pressure unless you are sure of your quantity of Coal carrying you to Halifax without drawing on the expansion."

Details are then given for measuring the coal. Three times a day, over a period of one hour each time, the coal to be burned was to be measured in baskets each containing about fifty pounds. An average of the number of basketfuls used per hour was to be taken for computing the daily consumption, the mathematics involved being carefully worked out for the captain's edification, even a table of cwts. and equivalent pounds being provided. The chief engineer either did not require such assistance or else was considered

incapable of the requisite mental effort. This
particular section of the instructions very
tersely concludes with "Burn up all the ashes,
throw nothing overboard. There are riddles on
board."

Of course, this serves to show how much is
learned by experience, but this is not confined to
the engineers but applies to all the other departments of the ship, the navigation, and also those
immediately concerned with the welfare of the
passengers.

It is a far cry from the beginnings of steam
navigation. In the old *Britannia* the engine room
staff consisted of the master engineer, three working engineers, eight firemen and four trimmers.
The *Aquitania's* engine room complement, in
1914, consisted of the chief engineer, thirty-
four engineer officers, twenty greasers, sixteen
leading firemen, nearly three hundred firemen
and trimmers, making a total of about four
hundred: but, of course, the coal consumption
of the *Britannia* was only about thirty-eight tons
per day, while that of the *Aquitania* was nearer a
thousand. To-day the engine room complement
of the *Aquitania* is considerably less, as would be
expected, in view of the introduction of oil-fuel.
As a matter of fact, the big staff of engineer officers
on ships like this includes several who have

nothing at all to do with the engines for propelling the ship.  The ventilation engineer is
fully occupied in attending to the air supply and
in seeing that the correct temperature is maintained.  Such importance is attached to both the
ventilation and temperature that charts showing
the position throughout the whole ship are brought
up to date hourly.  The deck engineers, too,
have little spare time, for they have to watch
over the hot and cold water supply for the
great swimming bath, the baths and lavatories,
the drinking water supply, the fire service and
hydraulic pumps, the dynamo and the emergency
lighting set.

Before running over a few details of the auxiliary
machinery and the electrical equipment on our
ship, I will give a few particulars of her four black
and red funnels, as these are marks of distinc-
tion by which she is known the world over.  Contrary to the general belief, they are not cylindrical
but eliptical, and without going into details of the
dimensions, it will suffice to show their enormous
size to state that a big railway locomotive could
quite easily run through any of them if they were
laid down horizontally.  Their height is nearly
170 ft. above the base line of the ship.  Their
purpose, of course, is to provide uptakes for the
fumes from the fires.  Seeing that the number of

funnels differ even on ships of similar size it might
be asked what determines the number. How
many are really necessary? As a matter of fact
the question must be decided to suit each particular ship.

The most economical arrangement, however, is
to fit one funnel to serve all the boilers. In the
*Aquitania's* big sister, the *Berengaria*—twenty-
four boilers are served by one funnel- one funnel
involves a minimum cutting of the decks and
therefore more space should be available for cargo
or passenger accommodation. On the other hand,
such an arrangement involves long passages in
the group to join the funnel proper. In small
steamers, like a cross-Channel vessel, and even
in destroyers, each boiler may have its own funnel, but such an arrangement is impracticable in
a ship with a large battery of boilers like the
*Aquitania*. Of course in some cases the number
of funnels is determined by the effect on the
general appearance of the ship, and this point has
such weight that we find a number of ships provided with dummy funnels. This is not the case
with the *Aquitania*. For the sake of appearance
the funnel to No. 4 boiler room has been made
the same size as the others, the additional air
space available beyond that required to act as
a funnel for the three boilers in the room,

being used as a ventilator for the centre turbine room.

*Electric Equipment*

Among other remarkable features of the *Aquitania* mechanical equipment are the electric lighting arrangements. They are sufficient to light a town of 100,000 inhabitants. Over 200 miles of cables have been laid, and over 700 miles of wires, weighing about 45 tons. In round figures 90,000 porcelain insulators were used in the work. There are about 180 separate motors on board, their total horse-power being nearly 2,000. Nearly 10,000 lights are fitted, together with more than 1,500 bell pushes. In the kitchens alone there are about 40 different electrically-driven appliances for culinary and cleaning purposes, whilst electric power is used to work fans, pumps, lifts, davits, deck cranes, clocks, thermo tanks, whistles, search lights, telephones, and wireless apparatus.

It will be recalled that electricity was employed even in the preliminary operations, a dozen or more electric derrick cranes being erected along both sides of the building berth. And when the ship came to be launched the same power was adopted for releasing the triggers of the launching gear, as well as the mechanism for breaking the ceremonial bottle of wine against the side of the ship.

The generating station containing big turbo-generators is in a compartment placed between No. 3 and No. 4 boiler rooms.

The main switchboard is 44 feet long, and the power is transmitted from the main switch-board to various auxiliary switchboards placed at different positions on the port and starboard sides. Cross-connecting cables are provided, so that in the event of failure of one section the supply can be maintained from the other side. The total length of the single wires amounts to approximately 135 miles, and of the stranded and multiple cables to 65 miles, making in all about 200 miles of cable. The gross weight of all the wires, including their insulation, is esti-mated to be about 50 tons, and the total weight of copper to be about 25 tons.

To prevent any possibility of failure of the electrical installation special precautions were taken in regard to the mains, sub-mains, and branch wiring, and the woodwork of the ship was speci-ally constructed to enable them to be easily acces-sible in emergencies. Time will not permit me to refer to all the applications of electric power on board, but the following tabulated list of motors which have been installed, and the

purposes for which they are used will serve to
show the extent and variety of the plant:

| | | | |
|---|---|---|---|
| 14 motors, aggregating | 700 | h.p. for forced draught. |
| 30 ,, ,, | 479 | h.p. for ventilation of machinery spaces. |
| 17 ,, ,, | 333 | h.p. for auxiliary machinery in engine-room. |
| 52 ,, ,, | 182 | h.p. for ventilating ship. |
| 36 ,, ,, | 205 | h.p. for thermo-tanks supplying heated air. |
| 5 ,, ,, | 42.5 | h.p. for 1st and 2nd class passenger lifts. |
| 2 ,, ,, | 60 | h.p. for lifeboat winches. |
| 4 ,, ,, | 46 | h.p. for electric jib-cranes. |
| 2 ,, ,, | 30 | h.p. for mail and baggage lifts. |
| 3 ,, ,, | 22.5 | h.p. for stores and service lifts. |
| 8 ,, ,, | 8 | h.p. for gymnasium. |
| 1 motor of 1.5 h.p. for sounding machines. | | |
| 1 ,, ,, 2 h.p. for gyroscope. | | |
| 1 ,, ,, 10 h.p. for deck winches. | | |

The total number of motors is 200, aggre-
gating 1,890 h.p. together with 700 h.p. for forced
draught. These motors range from a half to
50 h.p. each.

Along each side of the ship there are also ten
life-boat lamps, which provide light for the boat
deck: when necessary, these lamps can be inclined outwards so as to illuminate the ship's

sides. These lamps are controlled by switches on the bridge. There are also four connections for searchlights.

Many devices and appliances have been installed for securing the safety of the ship, and these are all more or less controlled by electricity. To detect any outbreak of fire the cargo holds are fitted with the fire indicating and extinguishing system, and in the passenger accommodation there are automatic alarms and numerous "break glass" pushes.

A separate circuit of 700 lamps is connected to an emergency set, these lamps being distributed throughout the public rooms and passages on ten decks, so that in the event of failure of the main generating plant sufficient light is obtainable to enable passengers and crew to find their way about. The lifeboat lamps and deck lamps, and, of course, the wireless apparatus are all connected to this. Under normal conditions current is supplied from the main generator, and when it is required from the emergency set a change-over switch has to be operated.

### Bridge and Engine-Room Telegraphs

The bridge and engine-room telegraph instruments are connected through hollow steel shafting with ball-bearing brackets and bevel wheels. The transmitters are fitted with a handwheel. An engraved plate on the transmitter shows exactly where the wheel is to be left at the completion of a change of orders. One revolution of this handwheel moves the pointers on both the bridge and the turbine instruments to the centre of the next order, and locks the pointer in this position. This is one of the principal features of the telegraph, which does away with any possibility of mistaken orders, as the pointers can only take up the mid-position of each order. It is interesting to note that the length of shafting between the bridge and turbine room in each separate lead is nearly seven hundred feet. The installation consists of eight transmitters: four of which are fitted on the bridge and four on the flying bridge, so that the turbines can be controlled from either station. The means of replying to the orders received is by a system of electric bells, a push being fitted by each indicator, and a gong at each transmitter. In addition, "telltale" instruments are mounted directly opposite to each transmitter. These are worked automatically by the propeller shafts, so that the commander can see at a glance the direction and speed at which the propellers are revolving.

The starting platform in the turbine rooms also carries four similar instruments. In addition to

showing the actual speed of the engines they also
indicate, by means of an additional pointer, the
direction in which the shafts are revolving, either
"ahead" or "astern." They have fitted to them
a counter, which records every revolution made
by the engine in either direction. Another interesting feature in connection with the telegraph installation is a device for warning the
engineer should the turbines revolve in a
direction contrary to that ordered by the telegraph; if this should happen a bell rings and
a red lamp is lighted. A telegraph is also fitted
from the starting platform to the boiler room.
There are a number of telegraphs which indicate
to the engineers by ringing a bell when the
boilers are to be fired, and show a number
indicating which boiler is to be fired.

The efficient ventilation of the engine rooms
presented a very great difficulty, but the careful
attention devoted to this matter by the owners,
in conjunction with the engine builders, resulted
in very satisfactory results. The ventilation plant
for the engine rooms comprises in all twenty-six
motor-driven fans. The large cowls up on deck
ventilate the engine room, and number in all
about thirty-three. The largest have a diameter
of 6 ft., with a mouth opening to 9 ft. in
diameter.

The whistles of the *Aquitania* consist of three
bell domes to each set grouped together, one set
being fitted on each of the two foremost funnels.
They are electrically operated, the officer on the
bridge having merely to close a switch to give
the blast, and there is also an electric time-
control arrangement whereby the whistles are
automatically blown at frequent intervals during
foggy weather.

The preservation of the perishable provisions
for the catering department of a large liner is
always of the utmost importance, and must have
careful consideration, particularly if the successful preparation of food is to be assured. The
refrigerating plant in the *Aquitania*, together with
all its accessories, is one of the largest and most
complete yet installed on any ship. The
machinery is situated in a specially-constructed
room arranged at the bottom of the ship, on the
tank top between two of the main boiler rooms,
and is capable of making about thirty tons of
ice per twenty-four hours.

For carrying provisions and other things which
require to be kept cool a number of special cool-
air chambers are provided. The main set is
situated on the orlop deck amidships, and consists
of twelve large insulated compartments, fitted
respectively to carry beef, mutton, poultry, ice,

fish, dairy produce, vegetables, fruits, wines and beer, each having a separate chamber or compartment, the temperature of which can be regulated as desired. The net storage space in the main chambers is over 18,000 ft. In addition to the main chambers, there are some twenty auxiliary cold chambers, pantries, bar refrigerators, and wine and beer coolers situated in various parts of the vessel. Several of the chambers are fitted with rails and hooks for hanging meat.

For the elaborate arrangements for operating watertight compartments and bulkhead doors, there is an electric system to indicate to the bridge which doors are open and which doors are closed. There is a similar indicator at the engine room starting platform. Another rather important fitting on the bridge is a patent automatic masthead and side-light indicator, which guards against a failure in the navigating lights. For communication with other vessels at night two Admiralty Morse signalling lamps are supplied, one on the mast head and the other on the flying bridge. The two whistles on the funnels, as already mentioned, are electrically controlled. An electric helm indicator shows on the bridge every movement and position of the rudder. The small electric motor used for the gyroscope is operated in connection with the instrument for recording oscillations of the ship, and the submarine signalling apparatus is electrical, receivers being placed in a small telephone cabinet on the bridge. Among other interesting appliances is a motor-driven sounding machine which indicates to the navigating officer the depth of the water.

Thirty-seven electric clocks, all the dials being controlled by a master clock placed in the chart room, are fitted throughout the ship. There is a master clock for automatically advancing and retarding the ship's time according to the longitude. Eighteen loud-speaking telephones help in the navigation of the ship, and the control of the main and auxiliary engines.

Each telephone is mounted on the upper and after-docking bridges within a polished metal hood secured to a brass pillar, the hood being arranged so that when open it forms an efficient windscreen. For the use of the captain, chief engineer, purser, doctor, chief steward and other officers, twenty-seven telephones have been installed.

In all ships there is a host of pumps of various kinds—among those in the *Aquitania* are main water circulating pumps for her condensers, auxiliary water pumps in the engine room, and also pumps for washing down decks and for fire hydrants. There are air pumps, too, to take from the condensers the mixture of air, water and vapour, pumps for forced lubrication and other oiling operations—there are fresh water as well as hot salt water pumps, and others for the hydraulic pressure necessary to operate the system for opening and closing watertight doors.

# CHAPTER IV

## NAVIGATION

THE duties of the executive officers call for men of the highest experience. Before a man can become a junior officer in an Atlantic liner he must first become qualified as a master mariner; and to become eligible to sit for his examination as a master mariner he must have served at least six years at sea, which means seven or more years in actual time. After obtaining his master's certificate, a young officer who is appointed to one of the Atlantic liners, does not immediately assume the duties of officer of the watch, but has to keep watch as an assistant to a more experienced officer. At the present time six or seven years may pass before this officer becomes a watch keeper in complete charge of the watch.

Merchant ships' officers have to maintain good order and discipline by example and character, and in addition to their vocational duties, must be able to exercise tact, and display great and lasting endurance. It has often been said that a good merchant ship's officer is born, not made. This is certainly true. When an officer is appointed to a liner company, he will find many conditions entirely foreign to his previous experience whether in cargo ships or fighting craft. But the main object of his work remains the same, namely to bring the ship safely to the end of its voyage, efficiently, economically and without friction either amongst passengers or crew.

All these qualifications have been characteristic of the commanders who have held the bridge of the *Aquitania* from the time of Captain W. T. Turner (Commander R.N.R.), who was captain on her first three voyages. Captain Turner first went to sea in 1864, and spent nearly forty years in the service of the Cunard Company. He was master of the ill-fated *Lusitania* when she was torpedoed off the Irish coast on May 7th, 1915. It will be recalled that he remained upon the bridge giving orders until the ship foundered, and was only rescued by chance, after having been in the water for three hours. In the opinion of Lord Mersey he "exercised his judgment for the best," and the report added that "it was the judgment of a skilled and experienced man."

The late Commodore Sir James Charles, the *Aquitania's* second commander, whose dramatic death in 1928, just after making his last home port, completed one of the outstanding sea careers of modern times, was for many years one of the most popular commanders in the North Atlantic trade, and enjoyed the esteem of many thousands of Atlantic passengers. When fifteen years of age he was apprenticed to a company running a large fleet of windjammers in various trades, in whose service he remained till 1887, when he joined the firm of Shaw, Savill & Co., eventually joining the Cunard Line in 1895 as fourth officer of the *Cephalonia*.

After working his way up as third, second, and first officer in the *Lucania*, he was appointed chief officer of the *Etruria*, and in 1904 received his first Cunard command in the *Aleppo*, which was engaged in the Mediterranean trade. Sir James Charles subsequently commanded all the principal ships of the line, including the *Sylvania*, *Slavonia*, *Carpathia*, *Saxonia*, *Umbria*, *Carmania*, *Lusitania*, *Mauretania*, and finally the *Aquitania*. For his activities during the Great War he was awarded the K.B.E. He had been promoted a captain in the R.N.V.R. early in 1914, and when he retired from that service in 1921 he received the rank of commodore. The same year saw his appointment as commodore of the Cunard Line. His death came with dramatic suddenness immediately after he had completed his last voyage in the *Aquitania* before retiring.

It was his 728th voyage across the Atlantic, and he was in his sixty-third year. He was in command of the *Aquitania* when she was brought to anchor at Cherbourg early on the morning of July 15th, 1928, after an exceptionally good run from New York, and as soon as he had left the bridge when the pilot had come on board, he retired to his cabin. Ten minutes later his cabin bell rang, and two officers who answered the call found him in a state of collapse. The two doctors on the ship were summoned, and it was found that he was suffering from severe internal hæmorrhage.

During the passage across the Channel he was in a semi-conscious condition, and as soon as the liner berthed he was removed to a nursing home, where he died shortly after arrival, without fully regaining consciousness. While the disembarkation of passengers was still taking place the commodore's flag fluttered slowly to half-mast, and a hush fell over the ship and the quay-side—the commodore, Sir James Charles, had passed away.

Soon after the death of Sir James Charles, the *Aquitania* was placed in command of Captain E. G. Diggle, R.D., R.N.R. Captain Diggle started his career at sea when, as a lad of sixteen, he was apprenticed to a sailing ship at Liverpool. He joined the Cunard Company in 1896 as third officer of the *Saragossa*, in the days when a ship of 4,000 tons was considered enormous. After serving in the *Etruria, Cypria, Ivernia, Lucania,* and *Sylvania,* he became first officer of the *Carpathia* in 1904, and chief officer of the *Carmania* in 1907. His first command was the *Cypria* in 1910, and he has since been captain of the old *Ausonia,* the *Saxonia,* the *Carpathia,* the *Caronia,* the *Carinthia,* the *Berengaria,* and the *Mauretania.*

A look round the chart-room and wheel-house of the *Aquitania* is necessary before considering in more detail the duties of the officers. In front is a row of intricate-looking instruments; behind is a curtained wheel-house, like a darkened deck cabin. Ahead, as one looks down, are the wedgelike bows of the *Aquitania.* Here are the appliances which give absolute control and ensure the safe navigation of the ship:

Loud speaking telephones to all parts of the ship—the fo'c'sle head, the engine room, the look-outs, and the steering bridge; telegraphs in quadruple to the engine room and docking bridge, indicators showing the exact position of the watertight doors in the bulkheads; indicators from the engine room showing the number of revolutions of the engine; diagrams showing various sections of the ship, which colour up immediately with a red light in the case of fire breaking out; compasses, instruments connected with the submarine signalling apparatus, and many others. The steering wheel can easily be controlled by one person, a single turn and the giant mass of 46,000 tons responds instantly to the touch of the quartermaster, even though the immense rudder is a distance of nearly 700 feet away from the wheel.

In addition to the captain, and staff-captain, there are seven officers in the *Aquitania*, namely:

| | |
|---|---|
| Chief Officer | Junior Second Officer |
| Senior First Officer | Senior Third    ,, |
| Junior First    ,, | Junior Third    ,, |
| Senior Second  ,, | |

The personnel in the marine department is completed with the following ratings, namely:

| | |
|---|---|
| Carpenters | Boy Seamen |
| Joiners | Masters-at-Arms |
| Boatswains | Quartermasters and |
| Seamen | Lamptrimmers |

The chief officer and the first officer, assisted by the junior officers of a ship, are directly responsible for the safe and proper stowage of cargo, stores, mails, specie, and baggage of all kinds. These must be so stowed, that the vessel will be in correct trim for sailing, and in a seaworthy condition as far as stability is concerned. They have to superintend the taking on board of fuel and water for domestic and ballast purposes. They are also responsible for the selection and signing on of the crew in their own department, and for all the appointments for various posts and duties, such as boat, fire and collision stations.

In the charge of the junior first officer come all navigational appliances, such as chronometers, compasses (magnetic and gyroscopic), charts, sounding appliances, signal controls, flags, fire appliances, life-saving appliances, distress signals, and many others. These have to be in perfect order before the ship sails. In port the junior officers assist the senior officers in these duties, keep records of special cargo, mails or specie received on board, and also help to make out station lists for the crew.

Before the ship sails the pilot comes on board for the purpose of giving the captain the benefit of his local knowledge of the pilotage waters.

Just before leaving her berth the officers take up their various stations on the ship. The captain and the chief officer are on the bridge, together with the junior first, and junior third officer. The staff captain is on the after bridge, senior second officer and senior third officer on the forecastle head. The first officer and junior second are away aft.

The ship having left the dock, the captain is in supreme command, and besides being responsible for the safety of the ship and all on board, is in a general way expected to be aware of everything that is happening on his vessel. On a steamer such as the *Aquitania* no definite scheme of duty in the shape of watches falls to his lot. When approaching the land and making or leaving a port, however, he is always at hand either on or about the bridge, supervising and controlling the ship's course. In thick or heavy weather the captain has a very strenuous time. Frequently for as many as forty-eight hours or more on end he may find it impossible to leave the bridge or turn in to bed.

During recent years the big Cunarders have carried, in addition to the captain, a staff captain, whose duties are similar to those of a commander in the Royal Navy, that is to say, on a battleship carrying a captain in command. He is the senior executive officer, and, under the captain, is responsible for the whole of the discipline of the ship. If required, he will devote his attention to navigation, but he does not relieve the captain of responsibility in this direction. The staff captain is assisted by the chief officer, who is also on duty during the day.

It is hardly necessary to define very closely the different duties of the other members of the personnel in the executive department, but it may be mentioned that the six quartermasters on the *Aquitania* take turns in steering the ship in two-hour spells; the boatswain and his mates take charge of the seamen; the masters-at-arms look after the gangways and the third-class decks; the lamptrimmers see that the ship's lights are trimmed and burning. A large number of the seamen spend their time at sea in keeping the ship clean, touching up the paint work, and generally overhauling her lifeboats, which include motor boats. Each night a section of them washes down and cleans all decks.

To carry out the routine of watch-keeping at sea the officers, one senior and one junior, are continually on the bridge, being relieved every four hours. They have eight hours off watch

PREPARING THE SITE: ELECTRIC CRANES AND PILING IN POSITION BEFORE LAYING
THE KEEL

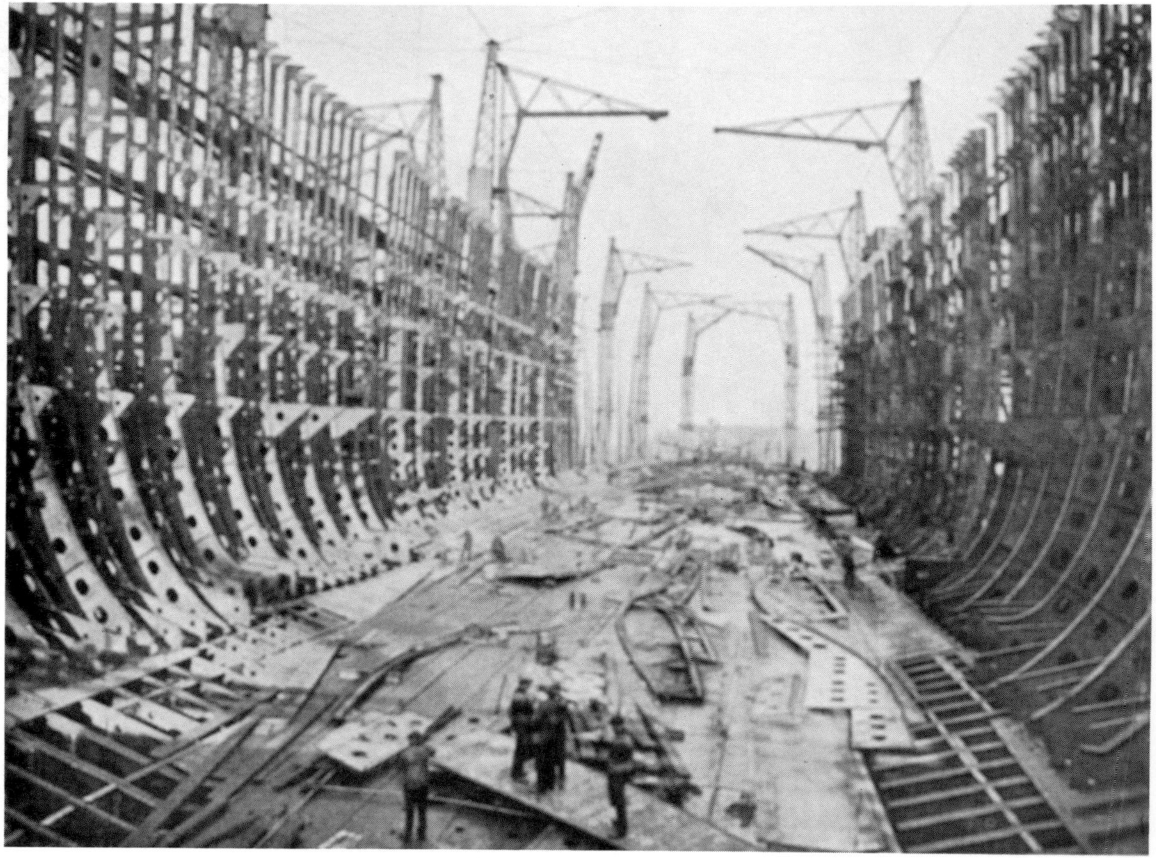

The Massive Vertebrae of the Hull Viewed from Amidships

A View of the Stern Frame, showing One of the Apertures
for a Propeller Shaft.

BUILDING UP THE SKIN OF THE SHIP—HYDRAULIC RIVETERS AT WORK

THE STERN, COMPLETE WITH RUDDER AND PROPELLERS, TOGETHER WITH NAME
AND PORT OF REGISTRY

A Close-up View of Propellers, taken when the "Aquitania" was in Dry Dock

On the Stocks Ready for Launching

A remarkable picture showing how this great ship dominated the landscape

CUNARD LINER "AQUITANIA"
Leaving WAYS — Entering WATER

SOME OF THE VAST CROWD WHO WITNESSED THE LAUNCH OF THE SHIP

The Gigantic Hull at last Rides Safely upon the Waters of the Clyde

CUNARD LINER AQUITANIA AFLOAT

Proceeding to the Fitting-out Basin, under the Charge of Tugs

A Low-pressure Turbine Rotor

The Complicated System of Dials and Gauges in the "Aquitania's" Engine-Room Starting Platform

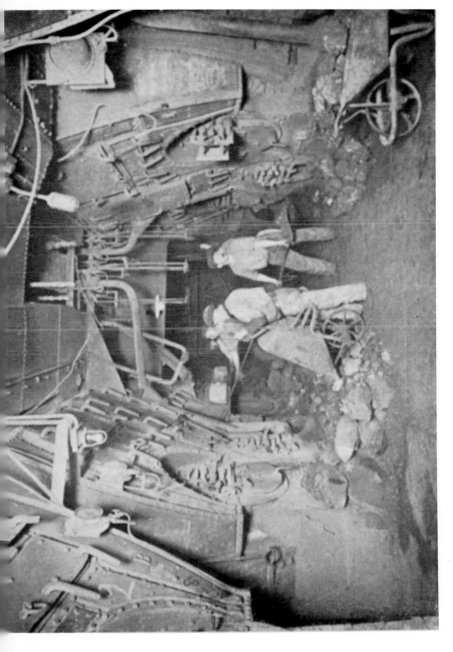

THE STOKEHOLD UNDER COAL-BURNING CONDITIONS

STOKEHOLD—AS AN OIL BURNER

Method of Bunkering with Oil Fuel Pipe Connection

A Study of Funnels and Ventilators

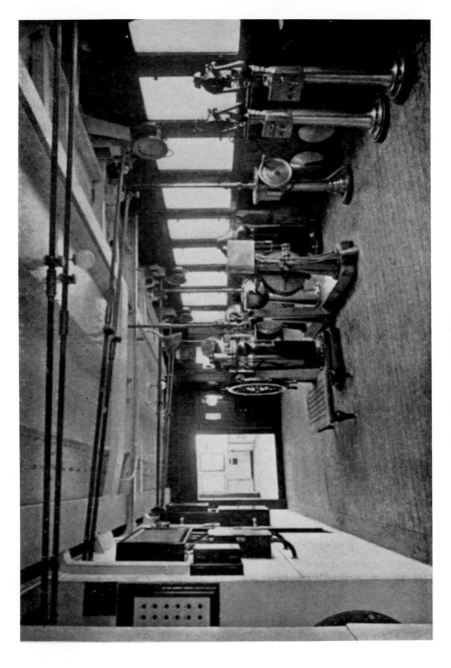

The "Aquitania's" Wheel-house

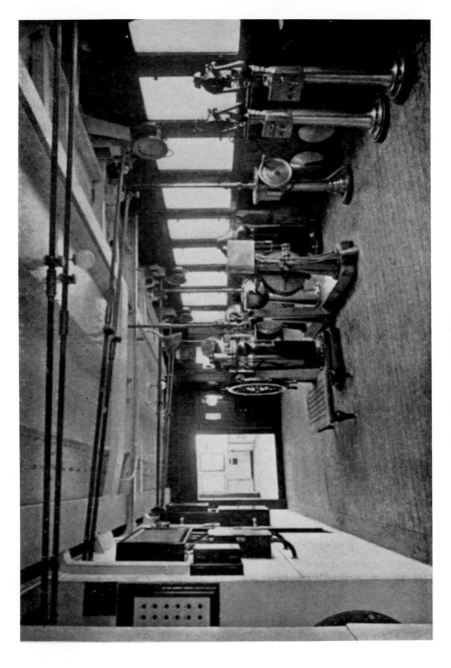

in order to perform their clerical duties, which
are numerous. This means that out of every
twenty-four they have not more than eight hours
bridge duty. In entering or leaving port, of
course, and in an emergency, they must all take
up their various stations as already indicated.
Further, when approaching port they must supervise the collection of the baggage and mails on
deck in readiness for landing. The senior officer
of the watch is in sole charge of the ship during
his period of duty, and is responsible for the
safety of the ship and all on board unless relieved
by the captain. The junior officer who accom-
panies him pays attention more particularly to
the steering, checking the compasses, and other
duties necessary for the safe navigation of the
vessel.

An officer on watch in a liner has to keep alive
to the fact that on his word an accident may be
avoided or incurred, and that he must be ever
ready to correct the mistakes or errors of judg
ment in others. Just as the navigating-house is
the brain of the liner, so the crow's nest might
well be called her eye. Here, high on the fore-
mast, perhaps 120 feet above the water level,
are perpetually stationed two look-out men. In
order to maintain that vigilance so necessary at
sea the look-out men have short spells of two

hours on duty.  On sighting an object the look-out man reports by a pre-arranged code of signals which, if necessary, can be amplified by telephone to the forebridge.  But an officer on watch has many other duties in addition to the look-out and any action which bears directly on avoiding accidents.  He must receive reports from the inspectors (ship's police), masters-at-arms, the ship's carpenter, and the stewards regarding certain details of routine in their departments.  At noon the steam whistle and engine room telegraphs are tested.  This is the end of a whole series of trials and tests of various appliances under the control of the officer of the watch, such as watertight doors, fire alarms, and steam valves.  Each watch, too, the compasses are compared and checked for error by the sun, moon or stars, according to the time of day or night.  Observations are also taken by the same celestial bodies, provided that the horizon is clear, in order to obtain the ship's position.

The hours of the watches are similar in nearly all countries and classes of ships.  Commencing at noon, the day is divided into equal periods of four hours, except that the period between 4 p.m. and 8 p.m. is divided into two "dog watches," called the "first dog watch" and the

"last dog watch." After 8 p.m. the watches
are known as the "first" (8 p.m. to midnight),
"middle" (midnight to 4 a.m.), "morning"
(4 a.m. to 8 a.m.), "forenoon" (8 a.m. to noon),
and "afternoon" (noon to 4 p.m.). Incidentally,
changing the clock in a liner crossing the Atlantic
is a much more complicated business than the
twice-yearly alteration of our clocks at home.
Between New York and London there is a difference in time of five hours, and as the sun rises
in the east, when the ship is going eastward she
meets the sunlight earlier each day, and her
course naturally causes her to gain time. On
the other hand, if the ship is sailing westward,
that is to say, with the revolution of the earth,
she lengthens her time, and the clocks have to
be set back daily. The length of time to which
the clocks have to be altered varies, of course,
with the speed of the ship. In the case of a
very fast ship like the *Mauretania*, for instance,
which makes the passage in five days, the clocks
would be set ahead or put back as the case may
be, about one hour each day. Usually the ship's
officers make the necessary adjustment twice
daily on a master electric timepiece which records
the alterations automatically on the other clocks
throughout the ship. Only the minor adjustments are made in the forenoon after the ship's

position has been taken, but the greater adjustments are made between 8 and 12 o'clock at night. These adjustments are so arranged that when the ship bound for New York arrives at Ambrose Channel light vessel the time on board is the United States standard time.

To describe in detail the advance in the methods of steering a ship during modern times would be beyond the scope of this chapter, but it is sufficient to say that the advance during the past two decades has been greater than during the last century. Up to about the middle of the eighteenth century a crude contrivance known as the whipstaff was in general use, and Drake probably used it in his *Golden Hind* and *Revenge*. By this time the larger ships of the period called for some form of improved mechanical device, whereby a considerable power, easily controlled, could be applied to the tiller—and the wheel was introduced. This was followed in turn by steam steering gear, hydraulic gear, and the hydraulic electric engine, till now we have a great ship's steering engine which is operated without human aid in a direct sense by means of the gyroscopic automatic device. To realise how great has been the stride in the methods of steering during the past fifty years, it should be remembered that in the 'seventies of last century it required as many as six or seven men to steer such ships as the *Minotaur, Black Prince, Defence,* of under 10,000 tons displacement, whereas to-day a ship like the *Aquitania* of 46,000 tons can be steered at sea by this gyro-acting device with only one man standing by, in case of an electrical or mechanical breakdown. With the gyro-compass, or "iron Mike" as it is sometimes termed, indeed, a far steadier course is steered by the ship than if the gear was operated by the hand of man. Only in exceptional cases can a man anticipate the movement of the ship and adjust the helm before the compass indicates that a helm adjustment is required. But with the gyro-steering appliances now available the most minute movement of the ship's head from its appointed course is anticipated and frustrated. What is more, the gyro-compass provides a permanent record of the courses steered in the form of a graph where every movement of the ship's head is recorded, which is often extremely useful for reference.

Although the gyro-compass is naturally superseding the old magnetic compass, especially in great liners, there will always be a certain demand for that time-honoured instrument. It is a curious coincidence that what is usually referred to as the "mariner's compass" makes what is probably its first recorded appearance in history in relation to soldiers. In the year 2634 B.C., a certain Chinese emperor, Hoang-Ti by name, was severely handicapped by fog when carrying on a campaign against the rival forces under Tchi-Yeou. One of Hoang-Ti's followers, however, hit upon the happy idea of steering a compass course in the fog, and by maintaining a general direction south succeeded in rounding up and capturing Tchi-Yeou, who was known to be falling back in a southerly direction. This story is probably more mythical than historical, but there is a written record of the existence of a "south-seeking chariot" in A.D. 806–20. It is also known that the Chinese had a south-seeking compass for steering their ships nearly 2,000 years ago.

The principle of the gyro was known to the Greeks, but the first people in modern times to attempt to adopt the gyroscopic principle to navigation were the English. In the early part of the eighteenth century a Mr. Serson tried to make an artificial horizon by means of a spinning top. So successful were his experiments in this direction that the Admiralty gave Mr. Serson permission to embark in H.M.S. *Victory* to obtain actual sea experience. The *Victory*,

however, was wrecked with great loss of life,
and Mr. Serson was never heard of again. This
happened in 1744. A copy of the Serson top
may be seen in the Museum of King's College,
London, and a good description of the instrument is still extant.

Great impetus to research work in order to
perfect the gyro-compass was given by the
submarines, for in a vessel which completely
envelops the magnetic compass the directive
force of the earth is lost or almost completely
overcome by what may be called "local
magnetic attraction" from every degree of the
circle. Herr Anchutz and Messrs. Sperry and
Brown, after much labour have steadily made
advance after advance, until to-day we have
the almost infallible instrument, which has no
variations, and is almost insensible to magnetic
disturbances.

It is interesting to note that the *Aquitania*
was the first British liner to be fitted with this
electrical compass. The principle of its working
would take too long to describe in detail. It
will be sufficient to say here that it is based on
Newton's elementary laws of motion applied to
rotating bodies, and is operated by the combined
forces of gravitation and the earth's rotation.

A gyro wheel is continuously rotated at a high speed, and tends to maintain its axle in a fixed direction relative to space. Various special devices bring the instrument to rest with the gyro axle truly north and south. The "master compass," as this instrument is called, is placed below deck, safe from weather, and where it is least affected by rolling. In the same compartment are placed the miniature electric generating plant, and a control switchboard for operating the system and transmitting the vessel's true heading to repeater compasses conveniently placed for steering and observation purposes.

Let us now examine how this electrical steering device operates in practice. Briefly, the gyro-pilot pedestal may be said to contain a repeater motor with necessary contact mechanism, and a reversible electric drive motor with sprocket and roller chain for driving the steering wheel. On top of the pedestal is an ordinary repeater compass for observation purposes. The function of the repeater motor is to transmit immediately to the contact mechanism, the least movement of the ship's head, while the contact mechanism controls the operation of the reversible motor, which in turn drives the steering wheel. The process is almost instantaneous.

Imagine now that the vessel is on her course and the helm is amidships. Let us then assume that the ship's head has swung off to starboard. Instantly, the movement is transmitted by the gyro-compass to the repeater motor, which, acting through the contact mechanism, sets the drive motor in motion in such a direction that the steering wheel is turned so as to apply helm. The application of helm will naturally check and then stop the movement of the ship's head to starboard, at which point the circuit to the drive motor is broken, and the steering wheel remains with rudder set to return the ship to the course. As the vessel commences to swing back to her course, the repeater motor—obeying the gyro-compass indication—causes the drive motor to rotate in the opposite direction, and apply the necessary "steadying" helm. The ship's deviation from her course or "yaw" is thus corrected very quickly by the automatic adjustment of her rudder by this wonderful device.

An officer is detailed for the special duty of seeing that the gyro-compass is in good working order. As has already been mentioned, there is a recorder worked on the barograph principle attached to the gyro-compass so that every movement of the ship's head is recorded. Frequently

during the day and night, or at least once every
four hours when any celestial bodies are visible,
the compass is checked for error, together with
the magnetic compass. Every hour while the
ship is under way the gyro and magnetic compasses are compared and the comparisons recorded in a book kept for that purpose in order
that if for any reason, either mechanical or electrical, the gyro fails, the magnetic compass can be
kept in reserve. Thus, in spite of the advances
of modern science, the ancient lodestone or
magnetic needle is still usefully employed as a
check.

Transatlantic liners follow certain tracks or
lanes, which are varied at times of the year in
order to avoid the ice which drifts south. The
majority of the principal Atlantic steamship companies have a working agreement with regard
to the tracks, which are known as A, B, C, D, E,
F and G tracks. The first three are on the New
York and Boston route and the remainder are
followed by ships sailing to and from Canada,
Nova Scotia and Newfoundland. When any
alteration of track is necessary the information
is promulgated to all concerned by the Cunard
Company, and, in addition, it is published in the
Admiralty and Board of Trade notices to
mariners.

The seaward and other movements of icebergs are observed by an international ice patrol, maintained by the United States. The ships and the personnel are provided by the United States, and the various countries trading to America and Canada contribute towards the expense of the patrol in proportion to their national tonnage engaged in the Atlantic track. Canada also has an ice patrol in the neighbourhood of the Gulf of St. Lawrence. The duties of the patrol are various, but their chief business is to locate ice and report by wireless to all ships on passage, and to the Hydrographic Department at Washington. The patrols commence their duties early in the spring, and leave their stations about the first week in August, when the ice is usually considered to have ceased to be a menace to navigation.

In most ships at sea frequent tests are made of the temperature of the sea water, with the object of enabling the navigator to find out whether he is likely to encounter any special current. This is possible owing to the fact that the drift and rate of the Arctic current or the Gulf Stream may be approximately estimated by the temperature of the water, thus assisting navigators with "dead reckoning." Water temperature has been found, after much experiment, to be of little use in indicating the presence of ice. Warm water is often found in the vicinity of icebergs, and cases have been known where a man falling into water between iceflows has found that it was like going into a warm bath.

Long before the days of international committees, safety at sea had been a subject of profound thought and research. It is a question in which Sir Walter Raleigh was keenly interested, and the family Phetts, father, son and grandson, devoted their life work to this end. Boat drill for the crew in a modern liner is carried out in port before the ship sails. In addition, the emergency lifeboats are exercised daily at sea. At New York boats are lowered and sent away for the purpose of exercising the crew at pulling and sailing.

Tests are also made, of course, with the motor lifeboats. An officer sails away in the boat and after tests have been made to the motor and other mechanism, a test is carried out with the wireless equipment. It is usually done in this way. The officer in the lifeboat sends a message to the liner concerning certain work that has to be done by a member of the crew. On the return of the lifeboat, the officer makes an inspection to see whether the work has been done in his absence, and if it has, it is proof positive that the wireless equipment of the lifeboat is working satisfactorily.

It is surprising how few people, even amongst experienced Atlantic travellers, could say what lies hidden under the canvas covering those rows of boats which form such an imposing wall on each side of the boat or upper deck of all Atlantic liners. They are generally aware of the fact that each certified foreign-going ship has to carry sufficient lifeboats for the number of people carried, that each lifeboat has to have certain tackle, and that lifeboat drill has to be carried out at frequent intervals. But their information does not go any further, although such lifeboats contain an orderly array of everything necessary to make the little craft safe for passengers should they ever be obliged to abandon ship. Elsewhere is a reproduction from a sketch by a junior officer of one of the *Aquitania's* younger sisters, showing a longitudinal section of a class "A" lifeboat, with the lay-out of the various things which the Board of Trade demands should be included in the outfit. And here is a brief sketch of the boat's gear, written in a simple manner, and leaving out, as far as possible, all nautical terms.

Each boat must carry a set of oars, two spare oars and one steering oar. The latter is easily distinguishable by its extra length, and a red band painted on the blade. Every oar is supplied with a crutch, which is an iron fitting shaped like a capital " U " with a vertical pin on the underside, all cast in one piece. It is more commonly known, though not correctly, as a rowlock. The crutches are placed in sockets in the gunwale, or side of the boat, upon which the oars pivot when in action. The crutch is not the only means by which the oar can be pivoted. There is the rowlock which is of the same shape as the upper part of the crutch, but is cut out of the boat's side, while the tholepins are two pins which fit into holes in the sides, and hold the oar in its required position. There is also a crutch for the steering oar, which has its allotted position in the stern, and also a wire grummet to keep it in position, as this particular oar is liable to jump out of the crutch by the rise and fall of the boat's stern. The steering oar is used to replace the rudder and tiller should the rudder be lost, or for any reason be insufficient to control the boat's direction.

A mast, standing lug and jib (or sails) are supplied for sailing purposes. There is a sea anchor in every boat, and perhaps it is the most difficult of all to explain to the uninitiated. Generally speaking, it consists of a canvas cone which in bad weather is dropped over the bows of the boat. The effect is much the same as that of an ordinary anchor, in so far as it acts as a drag, due to the water entering the wide mouth and being unable to pass through the narrow end. The result of this is that waves which tend to wash the boat broadside are prevented by the drag on the bows, and so the boat remains "head on" to oncoming waves, an essential position in bad weather. The rope which is attached to the mouth of the sea anchor is called the "cable," and the longer the cable the better effect the anchor will have.

Some eight feet from the sea anchor and to the cable is attached an "oil bag." This is a canvas bag stuffed with oakum and perforated at the bottom. The oakum is soaked with oil which, oozing from the perforations, has the effect of smoothing oncoming waves before they reach the boat.

Provisions are stored in the bread tanks, of which there are two. These are tanks secured beneath the "thwarts" (the nautical term for seats) and fitted with air and watertight caps. Though named bread tanks, the usual contents are biscuits, to the minimum of two pounds per person.

Water is carried in two water breakers, or casks, fitted on "beds" in the bottom of the boat. It would obviously be impracticable to attempt tipping the casks in a tossing boat to obtain the water, and so they are supplied with two "dippers," which are thin cylinders of such a size that they can be lowered through the bung holes and removed full of water.

In a locker placed in the stern will be found a compass and a tin containing a dozen red lights, which, after removing protecting covers from the ends, can be fired to attract attention. These red lights, or flares, are similar to those used at ordinary firework displays, but are of stronger power. This locker also contains one box of matches, more correctly called "fusees," which are enclosed in a watertight tin case. These fusees can be made to burn in practically any weather or the strongest wind.

Other gear fitted to each boat but of not such particular interest include a bucket, oil lamp, bailer (for bailing water out of the boat), oil-can, containing an extra supply of oil, and a spare plug for the draining hole in the bottom of the boat. There are also two axes, which are used to cut away any fouled gear.

An interesting point about the boat and its contents is that everything, to the smallest detail, complies with special regulations laid down by the Board of Trade, and is the subject of the greatest care and examination on board the liner. At least once every voyage every boat is carefully checked by a responsible officer, and a detailed record kept of their condition. It should be further stated that each boat is fitted inside, starboard and port, with numerous airtight tanks for buoyancy purposes, and these, with the gear and the boat itself, are periodically examined by the Board of Trade.

A new regulation recently put into effect requires all passenger ships to carry four certified lifeboat men for each boat carried. These men, representing all departments of the ship, are instructed and passed by the Board of Trade examiners, and with a view to meeting this regulation, such examinations have been held on all Cunard ships for some time past. The examination is not an easy one. All candidates are first of all orally examined in their knowledge of the boat, its contents and the various uses of the gear, and later on they have to lower the boat, hoist the sail—in fact, go through practically all that would be necessary in the case of "abandon ship."

To encourage efficiency in the manning and handling of lifeboats an annual boatrace between lifeboat crews drawn from the deck, catering and engineering departments of each ship is held. This race, which usually takes place when the liner is either at New York or Montreal, arouses tremendous enthusiasm, and the members of the winning crew are presented with medals by the managers of the line. In addition, a permanent trophy, which takes the form of a handsome silver cup, has been presented to many of the ships. This cup is held by the winning crew until the next race takes place. Although it might be naturally supposed that the seamen who comprise the deck department of the ship would always prove the victors, this is not so, for in many races the honours fall to boat crews drawn from stewards or from members of the engineering department.

Before leaving pilotage waters, or as soon afterwards as possible, the passengers are taken to their various muster stations in the part of the ship to which they would proceed on the "abandon ship" signal being given (this signal will shortly be of an international character so that passengers will be familiar with the vital signals wherever they may travel). When at their appointed stations they are instructed by one of the ship's officers how to wear their lifebelts, and how to reach the station in case of emergency. In every cabin will be found a notice giving instructions regarding the group to which the occupant of the cabin is detailed, together with the emergency signals and printed instructions regarding the lifebelts. Each stateroom or cabin carries the number of lifebelts equivalent to the number of persons in each room, and outside each cabin an arrow indicates the direction the passenger must follow to get to his muster station. Thus every step is taken to make the passenger familiar with the route from his cabin to the "abandon ship" station long before the ship sails from the quayside or weighs its anchor. There are two other forms of drill which take place daily—namely, the exercises for "small fires" (when hoses are run out and hydrants tested) and the "calling away" of the "sea boat's crew." The former generally takes place in the forenoon at different parts of the ship each time, and the latter in the first dog watch.

The dry docking of vessels of the size of the *Aquitania* is an operation which requires considerable skill from all concerned in carrying out the intricate manœuvres necessary. Prior to the vessel entering the graving dock, the bottom of the dock is "sighted"—hardwood blocks placed along the bottom of the dock to form a bed for the ship's keel, this work being carried out by the shipwrights. Four to six tugs, according to weather conditions, are required to tow the vessel from her berth to the graving dock, and approximately eighty shore-gang sailors are employed aboard and on the quay attending to mooring ropes and fenders.

As the water is receding from the dock a number of men in small pontoons, are engaged in scrubbing from the hull of the vessel seaweed, shell, and other marine objects which have adhered to the bottom of the ship during the period that it has been in the water since its last dry-docking. The hull, propellers, and tail shafts are then surveyed, and any repairs which may be necessary are put in hand. Before it leaves the graving dock the whole of the underwater portion of the hull is painted with anti-fouling composition, the total weight of which amounts to approximately five tons. The magnitude of the undertaking can be gauged by the high costs involved in dry docking and hire of labour, transporting to dry dock, including shipwrights' wages, hire of tugs to and from the graving dock, the use of the graving dock, and the cost of anti-corrosive and anti-fouling composition—which, at a minimum, involves an expenditure of £3,500.

Before closing this chapter a few notes on the regulations for the wearing of ensigns and other flags in a passenger liner may be found interesting. The following are the flags in general use in the North Atlantic services:—ensign, company's house flag, Blue Peter ("P" flag, International code), Royal Mail flag or United States mail flag, pilot's distinguishing flag, and quarantine flags. The blue ensign is flown when the captain is an officer of the Royal Naval Reserve or a retired officer of the Royal Navy, and the vessel has a necessary proportion of R.N.R. ratings serving as her crew; the red ensign when this is not the case. The ensign is displayed at the gaff when the vessel is under way, or whilst lying at anchor, or from the ensign staff when the vessel is moored. The company's house flag is displayed at the main truck (a small company's house flag is displayed at the jack staff on the stem head, but it should be noted that this flag is never flown when the vessel is under way).

The Blue Peter is displayed at the fore truck on the day of sailing, and when the vessel has finally got under way it is struck, and replaced by the national colours of the country to which the ship is proceeding. The mail flag is displayed at the port yard-arm of the signal yard, and signifies, of course, that either British or

United States mails are being carried. On the starboard yard-arm of the signal yard the pilot's distinguishing flag is displayed, different flags being employed to denote whether the vessel has an "appropriated" or a "rotary" pilot on board. An appropriated pilot is one who has been allotted to the service of one particular steamship line; a rotary pilot is one who carries out his duties on the vessels of any steamship line using the port. The quarantine flag, which is plain yellow, is only flown when the presence of infectious cases on board renders this necessary, whilst a yellow flag with a black ball in its centre is flown when a vessel has cases of plague aboard.

When at anchor or moored in home ports, vessels hoist their ensigns at 8 a.m. from March 25th to September 20th inclusive, and at 9 a.m. from September 21st to March 24th inclusive, and the ensign is kept flying, weather permitting, throughout the day until sunset. Whenever a vessel is coming to anchor or getting under way, the colours are always displayed, irrespective of the time of day, provided that there is sufficient light for the colours to be seen. In the case of vessels in dock at Southampton, Liverpool or London, the colours are struck at 5 p.m. except under special circumstances. When ensigns and

flags are displayed they are, on all occasions,
hoisted close up to the "truck" or signal yard.
The general rule is that flags should always be
broken after hoisting, with the important exception that the ensign is never sent aloft to be
broken. When colours are displayed at half-
mast as a mark of respect, the house-flag is flown
similarly, both flags being displayed one-third
below their trucks. It is always the custom for
flags to be mast-headed before half-masting, and
mast-headed again before hauling down. Similarly,
when saluting with the ensign at half-mast, the
ensign must be mast-headed first and again mast-
headed before being half-masted. There are special
regulations for "dressing" the ship with flags
on the occasion of the birthdays of the King,
the Queen and the Prince of Wales, the anniversary of the King's accession and coronation,
Dominion Day, and, in the case of the Cunard
Line, the anniversary of its inauguration on
July 4th, 1840. There is a prescribed method
of "dressing" ships either "overall," or "up and
down", but the various flag arrangements are
somewhat too elaborate to be explained here in
detail. The main difference between the two
methods is that in dressing ships "overall,"
the line of flags goes from the stem head to
the fore truck, then aft to the main truck

and from there to the taffrail, whereas in dressing "up and down" the lines of flags are displayed from the trucks, their lower ends being secured to belaying pins in the lee fore and main fife rails.

# CHAPTER V

## WIRELESS

In these days of radio, when shipping information is being constantly exchanged over the whole of the earth's surface, it is strange to reflect that little over a century ago the bells of St. Nicholas' Church in Liverpool were still employed to inform local business men of the thrilling news of the arrival of an incoming vessel. Another method employed by homeward bound vessels entering the port to announce their arrival was the firing of a salute of guns. At a later stage a rather primitive arrangement of signal poles on Bidston Hill, on the Cheshire side of the Mersey, came into being. Each merchant of importance had his own signal, and the moment the look-out man at Bidston could identify a ship approaching the river he would hoist the flag of the trader concerned. In this way the news of an incoming vessel preceded its arrival by several hours. The Bidston masts were largely superseded by the semaphore station erected in their midst, and by 1827 through communication by means of a chain of semaphore stations was established over the seventy miles between Liverpool and the look-out house at Holyhead.

But the birth of wireless telegraphy, by which signals are sent through space without the use of conducting wires, practically dates from 1896. In 1898 wireless communication was established for the Corporation of Lloyd's between Ballycastle and the Rathlin Island lighthouse, off the north coast of Ireland, a distance of seven and a half miles. In the same year Marconi installed wireless apparatus on board the royal yacht *Osborne*, in Cowes Bay, for intercommunication between Her Majesty Queen Victoria and the then Prince of Wales, who afterwards became King Edward.

These successes led to apparatus being installed on board the East Goodwin lightship, on the Goodwin sands, for communication with the South Foreland lighthouse, a distance of twelve miles, where it proved to be of great practical value, and opened up the possibilities of a wireless service between ships at sea and ashore.

In January, 1901, messages were sent from St. Catherine's, in the Isle of Wight, to the Lizard, in Cornwall, a distance of 196 miles. This success encouraged Marconi to attempt the more difficult task of sending wireless signals across the Atlantic. This was accomplished for the first time on December 11th, 1901, when signals were transmitted from Poldhu station, in Cornwall, and picked up by a station at St. John's, Newfoundland, a distance of 1,800 miles. An immense amount of labour, however, had to be expended before the initial success expanded into a regular system of transatlantic radiotelegraphy.

The number of passenger vessels equipped with wireless apparatus was increasing, and in 1904 the Post Office arranged to accept messages for and from ships, and so established a telegraph service open to passengers on board the vessels and their friends on shore. A certain amount of control is still exercised by the Post Office at the present day, for, before a wireless telegraph station can be installed for any purpose, either commercial or experimental, on board a British registered ship, a licence must first be obtained from the Postmaster-General. Each licence lays down certain restrictions in regard to the electrical energy and wavelengths to be used.

An incident which took place in 1902 served to bring home to those who were present at the time the reality of wireless. The Cunard liner, *Umbria*, on a passage from New York to Liverpool in May, 1902, had the American ambassador on board. This gentleman, during a speech he made at a concert during the voyage, said he hoped that, on landing in England, all might learn of the conclusion of the South African War. Late that night, in spite the fact that the vessel was far out at sea, a message was received stating that peace had been signed.

In the meantime, small-power wireless apparatus was being put into regular operation in the form of a system of intercommunication between ships and the shore. The small-power apparatus with which these shore and ship stations were equipped was only suitable for transmission up to three or four hundred miles under daylight conditions.

After the high-power plant at Poldhu had been brought into a condition suitable for a regular service, the Marconi Company organised a service of long-distance transmission of news to ships in the Atlantic, and the Cunard Line took the initiative in publishing small daily newspapers on board their chief passenger steamers during the voyage, containing news received by wireless the previous night. The first ocean wireless daily newspaper was published in the *Lucania*, the ship in which the Cunard Company first made regular use of wireless telegraphy. The *Cunard Daily Bulletin*, published on the *Campania*, in 1904, contained a regular service of news throughout the voyage concerning events in the Russo-Japanese War. The latest news, including market quotations, is now received by wireless throughout the day and night, and published every morning in the *Daily Mail Atlantic Edition*. The wonderful organisation which makes the printing and publishing of a daily ocean newspaper possible is described in detail at the close of this chapter.

Not so many years ago the commencement of a sea voyage for the ocean traveller meant isolation from his family and friends ashore and severance of all contact with the bustling world of commerce. The period of waiting was also frequently the cause of much anxiety to the relatives and friends of passengers. Today, though many miles of sea separate the voyager from his home and business, radio provides reliable communication with all parts of the world at any time of the day or night.

The art of wireless communication has developed to such an extent during recent years that it is now possible to receive messages under conditions which would have made reception impossible before. There are two kinds of signals which may be heard—telephonic and telegraphic: telephonic signals are transmitted from the many broadcasting stations which are now in operation; telegraphic signals are sent in Morse code, i.e. by means of dots and dashes, which have to be interpreted before the message can be understood. Thousands of messages are exchanged daily between the high-power stations of the world and between ships at sea in the Morse code.

The coherer, an early form of detector, was replaced by the Fleming valve on account of the latter's greater sensitivity. Further, the valve had another advantage, in that it could not be permanently injured or set out of adjustment by any exceptionally strong signals such as those due to atmospheric electricity.

In 1904 Dr. J. A. Fleming developed the thermionic valve. This valve was used as a standard detector for a number of years on commercial stations, but was later superseded by the crystal detector, on account of the latter not requiring a battery capable of giving a current of about 1 or 2 amperes necessary for heating the filament of the valve.

Although the Fleming valve proved a very good detector, it was not superior to a good crystal detector in its then state of development. It was not until certain improvements were made to it that it really became the remarkable instrument about which so much is known today. The main improvement consisted of the insertion of a small coil of wire which is called the "grid." This had the effect of making the telephones more sensitive to the signals received than was possible when using the valves as invented by Dr. Fleming. The crystal detector, however, has since been replaced by the three electrode thermionic valve, similar to that now used in present day broadcast receivers.

From 1904 to 1913 the thermionic valve was used only for reception, but in the latter year it was discovered that a valve may be used to generate high-frequency continuous oscillations, and thus become a powerful agent for the production of continuous waves.

Large transmitting valves are employed in the *Aquitania's* wireless installations for the transmission of long distance messages.

The development of wireless telephony runs along roughly parallel lines with that of ordinary telegraphic communication. By replacing the sending key of the telegraphic set by an ordinary microphone, the ether waves are made to convey speech or musical sounds just as readily as they had carried the "dots" and "dashes" of the Morse code. The difficulty which was experienced in the early days in getting enough energy into the ether to give a sufficiently long range to the transmitted message was overcome mainly owing to the superior merits of the valve as a means for generating the necessary power.

The *Aquitania* is now equipped with the most modern long-distance apparatus, capable of maintaining constant service in Great Britain, Canada and United States of America, and also with vessels at sea at all times throughout the voyage. This service provides a fast, reliable and economical means of communication.

The original wireless station installed in the *Aquitania* when she was first put into commission, though the most modern available at the time, would no doubt bring a smile to the face of an amateur in these days of valve transmitters and multi-valve receivers. The original receivers consisted of a magnetic tuner and multiple detector, the latter being a most complicated

GYROSCOPIC REPEATER, MAGNETIC COMPASS AND WHEEL

THE LATE CAPTAIN SIR JAMES CHARLES AND OFFICERS TAKING THE SUN AT NOON

THE LOOK-OUT MAN IN THE CROW'S NEST

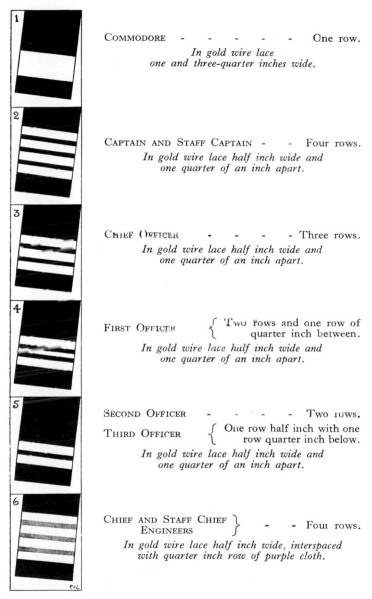

COMMODORE - - - - - One row.
*In gold wire lace
one and three-quarter inches wide.*

CAPTAIN AND STAFF CAPTAIN - - Four rows.
*In gold wire lace half inch wide and
one quarter of an inch apart.*

CHIEF OFFICER - - - - Three rows.
*In gold wire lace half inch wide and
one quarter of an inch apart.*

FIRST OFFICER { Two rows and one row of quarter inch between.
*In gold wire lace half inch wide and
one quarter of an inch apart.*

SECOND OFFICER - - - - Two rows.
THIRD OFFICER { One row half inch with one row quarter inch below.
*In gold wire lace half inch wide and
one quarter of an inch apart.*

CHIEF AND STAFF CHIEF ENGINEERS } - - Four rows.
*In gold wire lace half inch wide, interspaced
with quarter inch row of purple cloth.*

As the uniform throughout is precisely the same in cut and style, it is only by the gold braid and cap worn by the captain that the various ratings can be distinguished. The above particulars will enable you to recognise the different ranks.

ENGINEERS SENIOR SECOND - - Three rows.
   „      INTERMEDIATE & ⎱ Two rows and quarter
          JUNIOR SECOND ⎰   inch row between.
   „      SENIOR THIRD ⎰ One row and quarter
                       ⎱   inch row below.
*In gold wire lace half inch wide, interspaced
with quarter inch row of purple cloth.*

SURGEON - - - - - Three rows.
ASSISTANT SURGEON - - - - Two rows.
*In gold wire lace half inch wide, interspaced
with quarter inch row of red cloth*

PURSER - - - - - - Three rows.
*In gold wire lace half inch wide, interspaced
with quarter inch row of white cloth.*

SECOND PURSER ⎰ Two rows with quarter inch
              ⎱           row between.
SENIOR ASSISTANT PURSER - - Two rows.
*In gold wire lace half inch wide, interspaced
with quarter inch row of white cloth.*

CHIEF STEWARD - - - - Two rows.
SECOND STEWARD - - - - One row.
*In gold wire lace half inch wide zig zag.*

WIRELESS INSPECTOR - - - Two rows.
WIRELESS OPERATOR ⎰ One row with quarter inch
   (Grade A)      ⎱           row below.

*In gold wire lace half inch wide, interspaced
with quarter inch row of green cloth.*

Captain E. G. Diggle, r.d., r.n.r.
The *Aquitania's* present Commander

CAPTAIN W. T. TURNER, R.N.R.
Who first commanded the *Aquitania*

[*Photo: Russell & Sons*

THE LATE COMMODORE SIR JAMES CHARLES, K.B.E., R.D., R.N.R.

AN UNUSUAL VIEW OF THE " AQUITANIA " BY THE QUAYSIDE AT NEW YORK

[*Photo: Topical Press*

LOWERING THE LIFEBOATS DURING BOAT DRILL

PREPARING TO LOWER THE BOATS

[*L.N.A. Photo*

OFFICER EXPLAINING BOAT DRILL TO PASSENGERS WITH LIFEBELTS

A TALK ON BOAT EFFICIENCY TO MEMBERS OF THE CREW BEING GIVEN
BY ONE OF THE OFFICERS

THIS PICTURE WILL GIVE A GOOD IDEA OF THE GREAT HEIGHT OF THE FUNNELS AND
LENGTH OF THE SHIP

ONE OF THE MOTOR-LIFEBOATS

AN UNUSUAL VIEW, ILLUSTRATING THE GREAT BREADTH OF THE "AQUITANIA"

AN AERIAL VIEW OF THE "AQUITANIA" IN FLOATING DOCK AT SOUTHAMPTON

A Successful Stewards' Tug-of-War Team

[*L.N.A. Photo*

A New Rudder on the Floor of the Floating Dock at Southampton, while the Old One is being Dismantled

In One of the Wireless Rooms

COMPOSING ROOM OF THE " DAILY MAIL " ATLANTIC EDITION

[*Photo: Topical Press*

TRYING OUT ONE OF THE MOTOR LIFEBOATS FITTED WITH WIRELESS

piece of mechanism, consisting of a soft iron band
rotated by means of clockwork, the spring of
which was constantly breaking, with the result
that the operator was obliged to sit on watch
rotating the band with his fingers. This instrument, however, was afterwards replaced by the
crystal receiver—a much more reliable and simple
instrument, and one which is still in great favour
for the reception of broadcast programmes. Of
these the *Aquitania* carried two—one for the
reception of messages on medium waves, and one
for the reception of long distance news messages,
transmitted on a higher band. After a few years
of service this receiver was supplemented by a
Fleming two-electrode valve instrument, and
shortly after by the modern three-electrode valve.
Her transmitter, in the early days of wireless,
consisted of a 5 kilowatt spark and was, no doubt,
the most powerful of its kind to be heard on the
North Atlantic at that time. This transmitter,
though still part of the *Aquitania's* wireless equipment, is rarely used, except for the transmission
of certain classes of traffic, and for answering
distress calls. The spark transmitter was supplemented some years ago by a modern continuous
wave panel, and it is with the aid of this instrument that the greater part of the traffic handled
by the operators has been cleared.

During the summer months the distance of reception is sometimes lessened owing to the prevalence of atmospherics. These are due to electric upheavals in the atmosphere when charges of electricity accumulate in different regions, and, on reaching a certain magnitude, discharge. When these discharges occur they set up ether waves which, like those emanating from a ship's wireless transmitter, radiate in all directions and produce vibrations in any receiving aerial within range. These waves are highly damped and cause considerable interference to receivers.

As the waves sent out from an ordinary induction coil transmitter are similarly damped, this type of transmitter has formerly proved useful as an emergency instrument for ships. In the case of the *Aquitania* this has now been replaced by a quarter-kilowatt spark transmitter, also installed for emergency purposes in case of distress.

To keep in line with the modern practice of handling high speed traffic and of ensuring direct communication with both sides of the Atlantic, short wave apparatus has been installed in addition to the long wave installation. Multiplex working can be carried out by a number of operators working at the same time. It is thus possible for three distinct processes to be in operation simultaneously, namely (a) the transmission of wireless messages, (b) the reception of wireless messages, Press matter, weather reports or time signals, and (c) keeping watch for distress signals on a wave-length of 600 metres.

Originally the *Aquitania* only carried three wireless operators. This number has since been increased to eleven, and the continuously growing volume of traffic will probably call for further increases in staff in the future. These men maintain an uninterrupted wireless telegraph service day and night during the ship's transatlantic passages.

A central telegraph bureau has been established on board, where passengers may hand in their messages direct to a wireless operator who is detailed for this duty.

The radio service has been found to be a highly effective, and a practical business aid, and offers to business men facilities for keeping in touch with the markets of the world and their businesses ashore. Passengers travelling for pleasure, too, can keep in touch with their homes, exchanging greetings with their relatives and friends.

Hotel, railroad, and aeroplane accommodation can be now booked by radio in mid-ocean in advance of passengers' arrival. Theatre tickets may also be booked in advance by this means, and arrangements made for the hire of motor-cars.

Banking, the transference of money, and other financial transactions in all parts of the world, can be carried out through the branch of the Midland Bank on board the steamer, in co-operation with the liner's radio service.

Wireless is now playing a greater part in life on the Atlantic liner than ever. In the near future it is hoped to inaugurate a telephone service. A special telephone kiosk will be provided, where passengers will be able, during the voyage, to speak to their friends on any passing ships that may be similarly equipped, or to their friends on shore in the United Kingdom and the United States, just in the same way as between towns five or ten miles apart. Communication to and from the liner will be effected by short wave wireless telephony. On the land stations the transmitters and receiver are suitably connected with the land line telephone system. These facilities tend to reduce the vastness of the ocean, and serve as an assurance throughout the journey by sea that they are still within reach of their friends and business houses.

An important service has been rendered by wireless telegraphy in the case of accidents at sea. Upon hearing the "S O S" call all stations that might possibly interfere cease work, as this call takes precedence over all other signals. Ship stations fitted with direction-finding apparatus take bearings, and endeavour to copy the message. The signal is sent out on the ship's wavelength of 600 metres. "S O S" does not stand for any of the fanciful phrases that have been based on the same initials, but was adopted merely for its simplicity and distinctiveness. The signal "S O S" was preceded by "C Q D." The latter was derived from "C Q" which is the general call meaning "all stations." In the early days it was realised that while C Q was good enough for general calls, it did not express sufficient urgency for a case of a ship in danger. The letter "D," the international telegraph code expression for "urgent," was therefore added. The use of the distress call is strictly forbidden except by the captain's express authority, and is then permitted only in cases of urgent need.

It has already been mentioned that the *Aquitania* is fitted with a quarter-kilowatt spark transmitter installed for emergency purposes in case of distress. In addition two motor lifeboats carried by the *Aquitania* are fitted with small but complete and easily operated wireless installations. There is another type of signal which, while not a distress call, is a warning to all ships of dangers in the vicinity. It indicates that the station is about to transmit a message concerning the safety of navigation, or giving important information relative to meteorological warning messages. This warning is always prefixed by three "dashes" i.e. three Morse "T's," and is broadcasted to all concerned whenever the occasion arises.

The British and other principal European governments maintain high-power stations for sending out time signals and weather reports at certain times each day to enable ships on the Atlantic to have given to them Greenwich mean time, and also information as to weather conditions at various points. Wireless telegraphy, therefore, furnishes another invaluable service to the mariner in enabling any ship with receiving apparatus to pick up correct time signals which give the navigator an opportunity of checking his chronometer.

In addition to time signals, certain stations broadcast information concerning the weather and meteorological conditions. Ships in the North Atlantic receiving these signals can determine approximately the weather they are likely to meet in approaching the coast.

Along certain parts of the coast, and on some of the more important lighthouses and light vessels of the world small automatic transmitting stations have been erected. These stations are known as wireless fog signal stations, or wireless beacons, and usually transmit on a wavelength of 1,000 metres. By picking up the signals from these stations on the direction-finding installation (sometimes referred to as a radio compass or "goniometer") a ship may safely find her way under such conditions of fog as would render the ordinary lighthouse practically useless. Each wireless telegraphic fog station transmits automatically a characteristic signal which is distinctive from any other in the locality. Any number of vessels may obtain bearings by means of these special signals simultaneously.

Wireless fog signals are in some instances transmitted in conjunction with an automatic device, such as a submarine signal sound transmitter. This method enables the mariner not only to obtain the bearing by wireless telegraphy, but also to determine the distance of the ship in dense fog, within a limited area, from the transmitting station. The wireless telegraphic and submarine signals are transmitted simultaneously, and the difference in time of their reception, due to their difference in speed, indicates the distance.

In addition to the submarine signalling apparatus, a direction finder is installed on board. By means of these two important wireless and electric aids to navigation, the captain is enabled to determine his exact position in any weather and during the thickest fog. The direction finder is capable of taking relative bearings, with a degree of accuracy which does not admit of errors exceeding one degree, from almost any ordinary station within range, which may happen to be transmitting at the moment. The scale of degrees, like a compass card, is affixed to the instrument, and is marked from zero round right-handed to 360 degrees. Before the wireless bearings observed can be utilised, the relative bearing as read by the direction finder must be translated into true bearings, and for this purpose it is essential that close co-operation should exist between the wireless and navigation departments.

In the case of a ship which is moving through a dense fog for some hours when nearing the English coast, and has in consequence lost touch with her exact bearings, the captain is able to ascertain his precise position by means of the direction finder. The wireless operator will first swing the movable coil of the goniometer and search for the call sign of some known transmitting station. Suppose, for example, he picks up Land's End coast station—by carefully swinging the coil until the signals decrease in strength, eventually disappearing at a certain adjustment, and immediately returning to audible strength as that adjustment is passed, the operator can ascertain the direction from which the signals are coming. This gives him one bearing. A second and a third can be similarly obtained from two other stations on the coast, say Niton, in the Isle of Wight, and Ushant, on the French coast, and the intersection of the three bearing lines on the chart should show clearly the precise position of the ship.

At the present time there are three main systems of operating direction-finding stations. In some cases each direction finding station is fitted with transmitting and receiving gear and works independently. Alternatively several direction-finding stations (all of them usually near a harbour entrance or difficult passage) are linked together by special telegraph cables, being thus controlled by one station which alone is fitted with transmitting apparatus. The control station in such cases is not necessarily a direction-finding station, but may be an ordinary coast station. A ship in doubt as to her exact position sends out a general inquiry for the desired information. Two or three of the land stations promptly analyse the direction from which the inquiry signals reach them, and each informs the ship of its exact bearing from the station. And thirdly, where a ship requires a single bearing only, the vessel calls the wireless station belonging to the direction-finding station direct. The bearing, however, is calculated from the direction-finding station.

## Medical Advice by Radio

A recent important development in the use of wireless at sea is the standardising of a code by which ships can wireless for medical advice, in cases where the captain feels that a case is somewhat beyond his medical resources. The necessity for such a code on international lines was first taken up by the British Medical Association in 1927, and a committee was formed to discuss the matter on which the Post Office, the Admiralty, the Army, the Ministry of Health and the medical superintendents of the more important shipping lines as well as leading physicians and surgeons were represented. After careful discussion, a

questionnaire was drafted to assist the captains
to send out reliable and useful data when requiring medical advice for a particular case—an
elaborate code, in fact, which covered the whole
ground of medicine and surgery familiar to the
lay mind, and was capable of including every
possible emergency which might arise at sea.
This code was first put into operation experi-
mentally in 1928 in all the liners of the Cunard
fleet and certain other ships, when representatives of the Board of Trade, the Ministry of
Health and the British Medical Association went
on board to test the comprehensiveness of the
scheme at first hand. The code was subsequently
modified to a certain extent, and a few possibilities
of error were eliminated. It has now virtually
reached the stage of an international agreement,
and at the Washington Conference in November,
1927, it was laid down that radio-medical con-
sultations messages should be preceded by the
urgency signal.

It is most useful, of course, for a captain having
no doctor on board to know that he can ask for
medical advice by wireless should the necessity
arise, and the fact that reliable advice is thus
obtainable is often of considerable moral comfort to the patient. Medical advice may be
requested either from another ship carrying a

doctor or from a shore station. When out of range of a shore station, and seeking advice from a ship with a doctor on board, the captain, if he is not in touch with such a ship, issues a call to "all ships," and, if necessary, has recourse to the relay system, by which ships are requested to transmit the message until a ship with a doctor on board or a coastal station is reached. The messages must be sent in the name of the captain, or if the captain himself is ill and unable to send it, then in the name of the officer in charge.

Radio-medical consultation services have been organised in the United States, and in most European countries, and are freely available to all ships, irrespective of nationality. In the case of European stations, the wireless operator uses the prefix "S V H" if priority over all other messages is required (save those following an "S O S" call), and when communicating with American stations similar priority is secured by the use of the prefix "D H MEDICO." Seven stations have been organised in connection with the Radio Corporation in America, and sixteen stations in connection with the United Trust Company, or Tropical Radio Telegraph Company. In all cases the wireless operator has to give the position of the ship so that in serious cases the doctor can, if necessary, close on the ship.

The questionnaire or code system of case-taking can only be described in its barest outlines here. The system is based on a list covering all points that a doctor requires to know about the patient. This list is divided into several sections lettered A to V inclusive. Sections A, B, C, D, E, F and G contain fundamental points about the patient's condition or injury, such as personal description (whether officer, sailor, steward, or passenger, etc.), age, rate of breathing, pulse, temperature, onset of illness, etc. Sections H and I are key sections, that is to say, they contain a list of the principal signs and symptoms associated with an accident or disease. If these are carefully gone through and all the items selected which are immediately recognisable as a result of the examination of the patient, cross references can then be obtained to the later sections (J to V) which analyse more minutely the symptoms peculiar to the particular type of case. Plain speech is employed in transmitting the message, except where use of a foreign language is liable to cause confusion. It is thus possible for a captain who has very slight medical knowledge to be able to send out a fairly detailed analysis of symptoms which is invaluable to the doctor who receives the wireless message for medical advice. Even a brief explanation of the code is apt to sound somewhat complicated, but, reduced to its elements, it is not unlike the set system which enables a tailor to record a lengthy list of measurements for a new suit. The procedure is described fully in the official *Ship Captain's Medical Guide* which is prepared and issued by the Board of Trade.

From the early stages of its history wireless has probably found the most useful sphere of work at sea. Wireless at sea has not made the sea uninteresting and dull, but it has doubled its interest and greatly diminished its dangers. The feeling of security the traveller now enjoys on the ocean is largely derived from the safety that this mysterious means of communication has brought to those who cross the ocean. Successful navigation depends on a very high degree of mathematical precision. The enormous progress that has been made in wireless telegraphy and the regular broadcasting, as well as collection of weather reports, has undoubtedly added appreciably to the safety of the ship. And from the passengers' point of view it forms the only possible link of communication, and enables them at all stages of the voyage to keep in touch with the land if necessary.

It was the development of wireless telegraphy that made possible the production of an up-to-date daily newspaper in an ocean liner.

Just as when you are at home you look for the newspaper every morning, so when you are aboard the *Aquitania* in the middle of the ocean the *Daily Mail* is delivered to you with your breakfast.

Father will want to read of politics, or of the latest news concerning stocks and shares. You may be anxious to know how your favourite football team fared on the day before. You will find it all in *The Atlantic Daily Mail*, which is edited, printed and published in the ship itself while you are asleep.

Every great event which has occurred in any part of the world on the day before is faithfully recorded in the ship's newspaper. That, you may think, is a magical thing. It has been achieved only by the most careful and elaborate organisation.

All over the world reporters and special correspondents are busily engaged watching and recording things. Their accounts of those events are telephoned, telegraphed, cabled or wirelessed to Northcliffe House, London, the headquarters of the *Daily Mail*, and there, men who have been trained all their lives in such things, go over the reports and prepare them for transmission to the ships of the Cunard Line.

Four or five times during the day and night a long message is flashed on the wireless to the editor of *The Atlantic Daily Mail*, who travels in the ship. His task is to edit the news, and present it in the form in which you read it in your ocean newspaper. He may have in the course of the day half a dozen messages, each relating to one phase of the day's news. He has to arrange them in due order and see that the proper importance is given to every item that he receives.

The news organisation never sleeps. No matter where the ship may be in the ocean, or at what hour of the day or night it may be, there are men all over the world gathering news for you or tapping it out at the great radio station at Rugby. All the news of the world comes into the office of the newspaper on board ship just as it does on land.

But with all that wonderful organisation for gathering news, and sorting it out, and sending it instantaneously over the ocean for thousands of miles on the ether waves, it would never have been possible to produce a complete daily newspaper in the *Aquitania* had it not been for a machine called the Linotype, which was

invented by a diminutive old German whose name
was Ottmar Mergenthaler.

Mergenthaler left his native country in the
middle of last century and settled in Baltimore,
in the United States of America. By his inven-
tion he revolutionised printing, and if you go
deep down in the *Aquitania* to the printers' shop
you will find one of his machines clamped to
the deck with great bolts so that the linotype
operator may do his work even when the ship
rolls in a storm.

You have probably all stood at the window
of a little printer's shop on land and watched
the man pick up his type letter by letter and
drop it into the composing "stick" which he
holds in his left hand. That was the method
which Caxton used when he first brought
the art of printing to England in the year
1475.

Printers become very deft and exceedingly quick
in setting their type by hand. They are called
"compositors," because they "compose" the
type in the order which it has to follow. But
the printer of a newspaper has only a very short
time in which to compose his type. Something
important, for example, may be happening in
London, in New York or in Montreal. The
news is flashed immediately to the ship by the

wireless, and the editor of *The Atlantic Daily Mail* expects the printer to have his account of it set up in type within a few minutes. No compositor in the world could set by hand the thousands of letters which go to make up one single issue of a newspaper in the few hours which are available for the job.

That is where Mergenthaler's linotype machine comes in; for it does by machinery what the old-fashioned printer does by hand. It is what is called a mechanical type-setter, and it works more than four times faster than the fastest hand compositor who ever lived.

The linotype operator sits at a keyboard which looks like the keyboard of typewriters they use in offices, but on a much larger scale. There is a key on the board for every letter in the alphabet, and for all the figures and the full-stops, and the commas and the rest of the punctuation marks.

When the operator presses one of the keys, a little brass tab—which he calls a "matrix"—is released by a gate at the top of the machine and runs down a chute to the left hand side of the operator. At one end of the matrix a letter is stamped in what the printer calls "intaglio"; that is to say it is not like an ordinary piece of type, but it is hollowed out

in the shape of the letter the printer wants to
use.

As the operator presses his keys, one after another the little brass matrices run down the
chute at the side of the machine until a line of
them corresponding to one whole line in the
newspaper is complete.

Then Mergenthaler's machine does another
wonderful thing.

The operator knows that his line is complete.
He presses a hand lever which forces a jet of
hot molten metal against the "intaglio" char-
acters of the type on the matrices—remember
these are all hollowed out in the shape of letters.
The liquid metal runs into all the crevices of
the "intaglio" and forms into the shape of the
type required.

There is a peculiar alloy in the metal which
causes it to harden immediately it comes into
contact with the brass tabs.

Automatically the line of perfect type—the
printers call it a castbar or a "slug"—falls away
from the brass matrices. (That is why Mergenthaler called his machine the linotype—it makes
a complete "line o' type" at one operation.)

The "slug" is forced by the revolution of a
wheel between a pair of knives which trim it off
nice and neatly. Another turn of the wheel

pulls it into a "packer-arm" which drops it comfortably into place underneath all the other lines of type which the operator has already "set," and which will presently make up a whole column of type.

But that is not the last of the marvels of Mergenthaler's machine.

The "intaglio" matrices have to be used over and over again. So, while the operator is setting his next line, the machine obligingly sorts out all the used matrices and drops them into their original resting places at the top of the machine, there to remain until they are wanted again.

That seems to be the work of a magician; really it is a very simple process. As we have seen, the hollowed out type is at one end of the matrice. At the other end are a number of little notches like you find on a Yale door-key. Each letter has its own design of notches; the letter A in one form, the letter B in another form and so on.

The chutes in which the matrices rest have a design of "slots" at the top, and just as the matrices have their own design of notches so each chute has its own form of slots. The notches will fit only into their own proper slots. Thus immediately the type falls away from the brass tabs they are carried on an endless band to the top of the machine. They run along over the chutes and when the letter A, for example, reaches its proper chute the notches engage exactly into the slots and down falls the matrix into its place, there to wait until the operator of the machine wants it again.

That is how the type for the newspaper is set while all the passengers are comfortably asleep in their staterooms.

As the night wears on, and all the news of the day has been received by the wireless operators, edited, and set into type, the time arrives for the actual printing of the newspaper to commence.

All the columns of type are arranged and placed in an iron frame which is called a "forme". The editor decides which items of news shall go at the top of his pages, which in this column and which in that.

Just as the stewards are being called to prepare your breakfast the last process of *The Atlantic Daily Mail* begins.

The "formes" of type—each of them making a page of the paper—are placed in a printing machine. The blank sheets of paper are "pressed" by the machine against the pages of type across which ink is continually being rolled by mechanical means. That is why Caxton called his printing machine a "press" and why people still talk of newspapers as "The Press."

And so the paper is printed and ready for you to read of the important events which have occurred all over the world while your ship is a thousand miles from the nearest land.

The ocean newspaper may well be described as one of the romances of modern journalism.

### DIAGRAM SHOWING HOW A WIRELESS BEARING IS CONVERTED INTO A CHART BEARING.

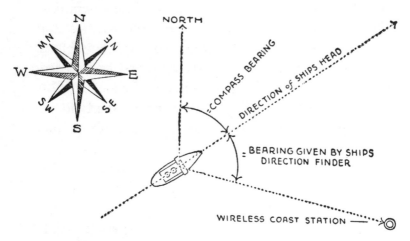

1. The direction finder gives the angle (in degrees) of the shore station *relatively* to the ship's head. (Hence, this is called a "relative" bearing).
2. The direction in which the ship is heading is known (by means of of the ship's compass).
   By adding (1) and (2) together, the "true" or "compass" bearing of the shore station from the ship is obtained.

# CHAPTER VI

## THE FLOATING CITY

As chapter succeeds chapter each thrilling stage in its history is being traced—from the vision of the men who first conceived the idea of the great vessel to the actual planning of the ship with all the wealth of detail which taxed the ingenuity of experts in every branch of marine architecture; from the laying of the keel of the liner to her launch, and then, later, to the momentous day when for the first time she set her bows towards the west and sailed in all her pride on her maiden voyage from Liverpool to New York.

And now there comes another stage in the story of a giant liner, the stage which tells of the fulfilment of the vision of her founders and of the pride of those hundreds of workmen who lovingly built the vessel.

But although the setting is in mid-Atlantic— the prologue to this final act is nothing more than an ordinary daily newspaper. For within its columns there is one of the most romantic paragraphs in the whole of the paper. This paragraph is headed "Movements of Liners," and somewhere within that column will be read:

"*Aquitania*, 1,500 miles west Bishop's Rock."

In that short line is contained a modern fairy tale come true. It is the fairy tale of the city which floats in mid-Atlantic.

Those who have seen liners lying in the docks, and alongside the quaysides of our great seaports, others who have seen them arriving from or departing on sea voyages, and those who have been fortunate enough to cross the Atlantic, will more readily appreciate the tremendous significance of that sentence. Imagine what it really means—

"*Aquitania*, 1,500 miles west Bishop's Rock."

With smoke pluming from her four great red funnels, with deckwork gleaming white and with hull black as night—except where her razoredged bows cleave the waters and white-capped waves race along her 900-foot length merging into a great wake named the Highway of the Atlantic—this great liner is steaming across the ocean.

At this moment she is practically half way across. Fifteen hundred miles away lies Southampton. At a similar distance New York, the mighty city of the New World is waiting. No land is in sight. On each side of the ship, for hundreds of miles there stretches the vast Atlantic.

On the bridge the officers of the watch, suntanned and bronzed are navigating her. Below in a strange world of living steel the engineers stand by the starting platform. By telephone and telegraph the officers on watch on the bridge send orders which reach the engineers at the starting platform.

Between the members of these two departments on whose stalwart shoulders devolves the immense responsibility of piloting the great vessel safely to her destination, there lives a population of happy travellers who are staying for a brief period in this liner which is the most luxurious and efficient floating holiday resort and city in the world.

That, in a word, accurately describes this wonderful liner. For she is nothing less than a self-contained city with her own reservoirs, oil-fuel and electricity plants, swimming pool, open air baths, gymnasium, theatre, restaurants, dancing halls, inns, verandah gardens, shopping centre, main and branch libraries, hospitals and dispensaries, cinemas, municipal offices, playgrounds, police force and fire brigade.

The "lord mayor" of the city is the captain. Under his leadership there is a body of ship's officers who are his tried and trusted city councillors. It is their duty to see that the city is kept in the highest state of efficiency so that all of those 30,000 visitors who stay in the city year by year will have a joyous and carefree time.

These councillors include the staff captain who acts as deputy lord mayor, and who in addition to being responsible for the running of the city, apart from navigation, also deputises for the captain at many of the social functions which take place during the voyage. Then there is the chief engineer who is the engineer of the city, looking after all water, heating and lighting arrangements, the doctor who is medical officer of health for the city, the purser who is town clerk, head of the municipal offices and the official "M.C." for the city, and the chief steward, who is a councillor peculiar to our city. He is in control of the vast catering arrangements.

The daily duties of the captain and his band of officer councillors takes them personally along the main thoroughfares and to public buildings to make sure that everything is in perfect order. In no other city or holiday resort in the world does such a daily official inspection take place.

As a holiday resort, the floating city is perfectly planned. At the outset the builders realised that all sorts of people, drawn from every walk of life, would often spend a brief holiday crossing the Atlantic, and that everybody would want to get as much comfort and benefit during their voyage as they could reasonably expect.

So this floating city was built in a series of terraces, all of which overlook the sea. But the higher the terraces went, so the accommodation for the residents improved and became more and more luxurious.

It is in this way that the residential quarters of the city are on the topmost decks. Here famous and wealthy travellers stay, and, as can be well imagined, the rooms in which they live typify luxury at its very best.

There are sumptuous flats which are absolutely self-contained, consisting of sitting-room, bedrooms, bathrooms, and a verandah; visitors can live in these apartments throughout the whole of their stay without as much as setting foot in the city. From their own private verandah they can look out across the ocean or watch the ever-changing pageant of people, promenading up and down as if in a park.

Then there are other bedrooms, all of which are luxuriously furnished with delightful beds, comfortable chairs, hot and cold running water, wardrobes, and to complete the last comfort, cunning lights over each bed so that one can lie in state and read to one's heart's content. Many of these rooms have private bathrooms adjoining.

There is also a simply limitless restaurant, where about 700 people can be served at the same time. This vast room is fitted with small tables, so that small parties of friends can have their meals together. Adjoining this restaurant is a smaller restaurant which is known as a grill room.

The smoking-room, which is the principal inn of the city, is a very jolly place which, with its oak-beamed ceiling and leaded window panes, gives a delightful atmosphere of England in the days of the stage coaches and highwaymen. And to complete the illusion, a full length portrait of King James II hangs over the fireplace.

From the tavern leads the long gallery or High Street. This is the great shopping centre of the city.

Quite recently a branch store of one of the most famous firms of gentlemen's outfitters was opened in the street. Here visitors can buy ready-to-wear suits, and fashionable designs in shirts, pyjamas, ties, or socks, and other articles of wearing apparel are displayed in the windows of this delightful establishment so that male visitors are able to boast to their friends about "my Atlantic tailor."

But this is not the only shop. Several other firms have large showcases close by. The fancy goods shop, for instance, is a favourite place for the lady visitors. And they spend many hours in choosing dainty handbags, cigarette cases and holders, and perfumery to take home as souvenir presents for their friends.

Then there is a chocolate and sweet shop, the favourite haunt of the "flappers" who visit the town. Tobacco, cigarettes and cigars can be obtained from another window, whilst visitors who are fond of reading can browse amongst the best sellers and thrillers to be found at the bookstall.

But perhaps the most enterprising shop of all is the jeweller's store. For in addition to bracelets, brooches, watches and other articles of jewellery, there is an adequate supply of engagement rings.

One unique thing about the street is that there is no traffic. Everybody can shop in the utmost comfort. Indeed opposite the shops, which line one side of the street only, there are tables and comfortable settees. So that while mother chooses her goods, father can sit and take his ease while enjoying a cup of coffee, or playing a quiet hand of cards with some of his fellow voyagers.

At the other end of the High Street is the main lounge. This is a truly glorious room, and is the public meeting place of the floating city. In this way it corresponds to the great concert rooms in the majority of town halls in cities ashore.

But the similarity stops there, because this public hall of the city afloat is furnished on a scale of tremendous luxury. There is a gloriously thick carpet running the length of the floor. There is a magnificent domed ceiling, and the chairs and settees are upholstered in costly fabrics.

It is here that the most important ceremonies and meetings take place. On Sunday morning it becomes a church. There is something so impressive and grand in the Sunday morning service in the city afloat that many will be found at the service.

The great floating city is steaming ahead. Through the windows of the "church" the tumbling waters of the Atlantic can be seen. Inside the church the congregation are reverently seated. The sonorous voice of the purser reading the Lessons for the day echoes round the room. The congregation rises whilst the captain conducts prayers, and

there is something really solemn and appealing in
the special prayer for "those at sea." The
service concludes with the singing of a hymn by
the choir composed of members of the ship's
crew, who are, of course, the permanent population of the city.

In this magnificent room the ship's concert
takes place. This is a brilliant event. Every
passenger makes a point of attending and at the
end of the concert a collection is taken, the proceeds
being given to various seamen's charities. No
finer cause could be found than that of support-
ing the widows and children of brave sailors who
have lost their lives at sea.

The concerts are very jolly. One of the most
influential passenger residents usually presides;
indeed there was one memorable occasion when the
Prime Minister of England took the chair.

Then there is no lack of artistes. For visitors
to the city very often include famous opera
singers, musicians and theatrical stars, who wil-
lingly give their services free. Sometimes a
famous explorer will talk about his most recent
voyage of discovery, whilst at other times an
entire theatrical company will stage and produce
a popular play.

The second half of the programme is often
devoted to a cinema show. This is greatly

appreciated by the younger members of the audience, who will be regaled with up-to-date comedies, news items and a thrilling big picture featuring the most popular film stars of the day.

On each side of the great concert hall lounge are verandah gardens. These are the most popular places in the city. All day long they are filled with the fragrance of lovely flowers tended by the gardener. In the morning these verandahs, which overlook the sea, are a colourful pageant of people. Some are sitting down quietly reading or taking their morning soup. Others are happily promenading, gaily chatting. In the evening the verandahs are transformed into glorious ballrooms. Hundreds of multi-coloured fairy lamps shed their soft radiance on the forms of beautiful women gloriously gowned and handsome men in immaculate evening dress, who dance the hours away to the music provided by jolly orchestras.

Writing letters is always a bore. But in case some of the visitors in the city want to write there is a special place provided for them. Here they can buy postage stamps and post their letters, so that this room might well be called the general post office. Still it is as unlike a post office as anyone could imagine. Visitors don't have to

H.R.H. The Prince of Wales on the Bridge of the " Aquitania "
DURING A VISIT TO SOUTHAMPTON

ST. JAMES' PALACE.
S.W.1.

30th June, 1924.

My dear Sir Thomas,

    Please convey to your fellow-directors of the
Cunard Steamship Company my sincere thanks for the
hospitality shown me on board the "Aquitania" at Southampton
last Friday.

    I was so glad to have a chance of going round
this splendid ship and was most interested in all I saw.

               Yours very truly

               Edward P

Sir T. Royden, Bart., C.H.,
   Cunard Steamship Company.

FACSIMILE LETTER RECEIVED AFTER HIS VISIT

The Fireplace in the Carolean Smoking Room of the "Aquitania"

THE ELIZABETHAN GRILL ROOM

One of the "Aquitania's" Luxurious Bedrooms

THE "AQUITANIA" IN "KHAKI" AND UNDER ESCORT

The Louis XVI Dining Saloon

THE FAMOUS PALLADIAN LOUNGE

SWIMMING POOL AND GYMNASIUM

THE STATELY SMOKING ROOM OF THE SHIP

A Transverse Section of the "Aquitania," illustrating the Internal Arrangements

A Sketch Contrasting the Relative Sizes of the "Aquitania" and the Tower Bridge

A ROUND WITH THE GLOVES ON DECK

A GAME OF PING PONG, WITH AFTERNOON TEA

Not Flies round a Jam Pot, but Workmen Putting the Familiar Red Paint
on Cunard Funnels

Mr. J. Lawler, the " Aquitania's " Purser

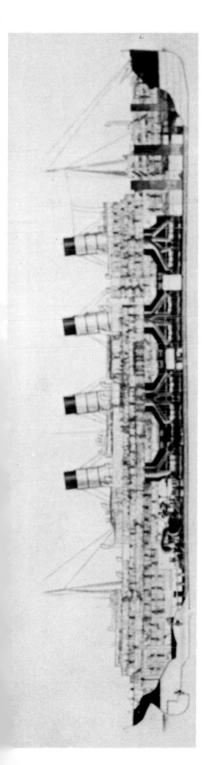

A Longt'' dinal Section of the Ship indicating the Tremendous Amount of Space Occupied by Her Powerful Machinery

Comparison of Sizes—" Aquitania," " Britannia " (1840) and the " Mayflower " of the Pilgrim Fathers (1620)

ON WITH THE DANCE—AN ATLANTIC FOXTROT

A BOLSTER BAR CONTEST

stand to write their letters. They are provided
with comfortable tables and chairs, whilst plenty
of notepaper, envelopes and postcards is supplied.
Strangely enough, this room is very popular,
especially amongst the ladies, and the average
number of postcards written daily by some of the
passengers reaches nearly fifty.

Adjoining the writing-room-post office is the
library. This is a square room, the walls of
which are lined with hundreds of books. One of
the pleasantest things about this library is the fact
that one has not to pay anything to borrow the
books. And as everybody likes the idea of getting something for nothing, one can well imagine
how popular the place is. Sometimes the poor
librarian has to bear with people who ask him
all sorts of silly questions. Some visitors ask
for books which they have seen other people reading, and when the librarian asks for the name of
the books they admit that they don't know but
that it had a green back! Others get the names
of the authors mixed up. Then there are people
who ask for a book that they will like without
giving the librarian any inkling as to whether
they like thrillers or love stories or adventure
yarns.

Boys have not been forgotten, and there is
a section of the library specially devoted

to adventure tales, school tales and detective yarns.

One of the great things people look forward to when they go on their holidays is the opportunity they will have of playing games. Visitors to the floating city are certainly not disappointed in this respect.

The playing-fields of this city afloat are wide and extensive. There is not only plenty of room for people to sit down and enjoy the bracing air of the Atlantic but also heaps of space for all manner of games.

Easily the most popular game is tennis. The courts overlook the Atlantic, and are occupied by enthusiasts from early morning till late at night. "Atlantic" tennis differs slightly from shore tennis. The courts are marked out in the same way, ordinary nets are used and the scoring is identical, but here the similarity stops. The players do not use racquets, and in place of the tennis balls which would, of course, be liable to bounce into the sea, a hard rubber ring is used. This is served by the one player and caught by the other player standing on the other side of the net. The game is really much faster than shore tennis; and the kings and queens of Wimbledon who have stayed in the city have played the game with delight.

Golfing enthusiasts find the miniature putting green a constant source of pleasure, and world famous golf champions, both professional and amateur, have assiduously practised here during their Atlantic trip.

Facilities for bathing are unexcelled. In addition to the canvas open-air baths there is a magnificent swimming pool below decks. The idea for the construction of this bath was actually taken from Egyptian ornaments in the British Museum. The walls of the pool are lined with blue tiles, and there are steps down into the water. At the side there are dressing-rooms, with hot and cold showers, all in readiness for when one comes out from one's swim.

And if, after a swim, one still wants more exercise, there is a gymnasium next door. Here many happy hours can be spent. There are parallel and horizontal bars, electric cycling machines, horse-riding machines, which will give the same exercise as if one were mounted on a horse, camel-riding machines, rowing machines, massage machines, fencing sticks, boxing gloves, punch balls, foils, and much else besides, with an expert gymnastic instructor to help to keep one fit and improve one's physical development.

Then there are other less exacting sports which crowd the hours of the day. One of these is horse racing, and it is one of the most accomodating kinds of racing in the history of the Turf, because if the weather is cold or inclement, the race meeting is adjourned to a comfortable place indoors, so that there are unprecedented occasions when a race takes place down the main street of the city.

This is no ordinary racing, with flesh and blood horses. As a matter of fact, the horses are carved in wood, and they are moved by hand along squares marked out on deck, according to the number given on a dice shaken by the starter.

Many other games there are to delight the heart of the traveller. "Are you there, Mike," is very good fun, and is played by two men who, blindfolded and holding in one hand a roll of paper, clasp their free hands together and try and find each other to the accompaniment of thwacks from the rolls of paper. Pillow fights are fought astride booms placed across the open air baths. "Giant holo" and "shuffleboard" are other games which provide plenty of amusement.

But perhaps the most exciting day of all is sports day. The whole city joins in this event.

Races of every description are held. There are
obstacle races and sack races for the hefty young
fellows, egg-and-spoon races and potato races for
the kiddies, a veteran race for fathers and mothers,
three-legged races for everybody, and, as can
be well imagined, the fun waxes fast and furious.
Generally sports day winds up with a gigantic
carnival dinner and dance. The floating city
is a blaze of light from stem to stern. All the
visitors wear fancy dress, which they have in-
geniously contrived to fashion out of all sorts of
odds and ends. The walls of the restaurant are
wonderfully festooned, coloured balloons of every
size and colour hang from the ceiling, and high
revelry is held until the early hours of the morning.

One must remember that this great city afloat
is just like any city ashore. There are the people
who are very rich, and who stay in the most
select and exclusive districts of the city. There
are also other visitors who cannot afford quite
such luxurious apartments in the city afloat.
These people can stay in any of three districts;
the "second class" district, the "tourist
third cabin" district or the "third class"
district.

Visitors who travel "second class" live at the
stern end of this floating city. They have lovely

apartments and comfortable bedrooms. There is a special restaurant, an inn, a concert hall lounge, a verandah garden, a library and writing-room and plenty of space for playing games.

In the same way the "tourist third cabin" visitors are sure of plenty of enjoyment. These "tourist third cabin" visitors have only come to stay in the city during the past two years. They are people who, having heard all about the city afloat, wanted very much to spend a holiday crossing the Atlantic. And so a special residential section was built in the city which would suit the pockets of these people, for not all of them were rich. Many of them are clerks who have still their way to make in the world, whilst others are young students and university graduates who find an Atlantic trip a topping way of spending their holiday.

The "third class" district of the city is at the forward end of the ship. But it must not be imagined that because of its name it is very terrible and dreary. It certainly is not. One would be surprised indeed at the type of people who live in the "third class" district, and no one need be ashamed of living there. There are cosy bedrooms, which indeed are considerably better than the first class staterooms in the very first Atlantic liners. There is an inn, a restaurant, a library and writing-room, a concert lounge, and lots of deck space for the visitors to play games.

And even yet we have not exhausted the wonders of this city afloat. For there are many additional amenities which help to keep the visitors happy and satisfied.

For instance, visitors to the city do not lack for news. There is the *Daily Mail Atlantic Edition* printed and published in the city. In the columns of this paper father can read and keep in touch with events which are taking place in all parts of the world, and mother can learn all about the latest developments in the world of fashion. Boys find this paper of interest because during the winter they are able to follow the fortunes of football teams, whilst in the summer season county cricket scores are given daily. American boys, also, who visit the city are kept supplied with news of their baseball teams.

Then there is situated in the city a branch of one of the most famous of English banks—the Midland Bank Ltd. Here a staff of clerks are on duty to attend to all monetary transactions. One of the principal duties which they perform is that of changing money, and as visitors to the city are of all nationalities, one can well imagine that the currencies of half the nations in the world must pass over the counter.

Visitors to the city who fail to have their hair cut before they set sail have no cause for worry. Luxurious and magnificent hairdressing saloons are to be found in the city, where they can have their locks shorn, trimmed, shampooed, singed, or attended to in whatever way they wish. And in these modern days, when mothers and daughters pay regular visits to hairdressers, provision has been made in the city afloat for these members of the fair sex to enjoy a haircut and indulge in a beauty treatment at the hands of a staff of lady assistants specially employed to cater to their needs.

Even in the best of cities accidents are liable to happen, and this fact has been fully recognised in the city afloat. Accordingly there are provided for the visitors who should have the misfortune to fall ill or meet with accidents comfortable hospitals and dispensaries, where they will be sure of the finest treatment possible at the hands of highly skilled doctors and nurses. Provision for every contingency is made, and cases ranging from ordinary sea-sickness to acute appendicitis, from a sprained ankle to the welcoming of a baby into the world have passed through the hospitals maintained in the city afloat.

So also, in an entirely different way, is the

safety of the visitors provided for, and to an extent that is not excelled on land. From the safety valves of the engines to the elaborate apparatus on the navigating bridge the word "safeguard" is spelled out in every single detail. Nothing is overlooked which might jeopardise the safety of the visitors, and although the risk of fire is greatly minimised, there is a regular fire brigade, comprised of members of the crew.

Then there is the city police force. Fortunately the "Arm of the Law" is not often needed. There is no traffic, and so policemen are not needed for "point duty." The citizens are so orderly and law-abiding that the actual name "police" has been dispensed with. Instead the city "police" are called "ship's inspectors." On sailing day they are on duty at the gangways leading to the city. During the trip they patrol the decks to see that everything is in order, and that no boys are getting into mischief by climbing the rigging or balancing precariously on the rails, sublimely unconscious of the drop many feet below into the Atlantic.

There is also in the city afloat a permanent population, the officers and crew—from the captain down to the newest greenhorn of a bright buttoned "bellboy"—who have but one aim and object, and that is to try to anticipate every wish of the visitors who stay in their city.

Nothing that the visitors reasonably demand or require is overlooked, and during the trip every member of the crew sees that visitors have a really jolly time.

For the permanent population is possessed to an extraordinary degree of that spirit which a boy has for his school, for his favourite football team, for his cricket county and for his native town. And this *esprit de corps* is found in the staunch pride they hold in the floating city of which they are citizens. They have their football and cricket teams, which compete with teams of other floating cities. They have boxing matches. And when in America, they arrange for picnics and excursions to neighbouring places of interest.

In their own comfortable apartments they have a special library of their own. Sailors are voracious readers, and this library is a very popular institution.

During the trip some of them attend school. Here they are given lessons by one of the officers in the handling and navigation of lifeboats. Then the bellboys and young commis-waiters are taken in hand by the gymnastic instructor, and are put through a course of physical jerks in order to keep them fit and well.

At other times these seamen citizens indulge in their own personal hobbies, for the majority of sailors are very versatile fellows. One of the most popular hobbies is the making of model ships. This is a very intricate art. For it not only requires keen eyesight, but also infinite patience in the piecing together of small cotton threads and fragments of wood which are needed for the stays and spars of an accurate model of an old schooner or frigate.

Very often they are able to turn their hobbies to profitable account. There is a steward who regularly crosses the Atlantic who is an expert clockmaker. Passengers eagerly buy his clocks to form a permanent souvenir of their trip. In another floating city there is a member of the crew who is an expert cartoonist. Travellers who have been the subjects of his facile pen greatly prize his caricatures.

Barbers and members of the orchestras usually adopt photography as their pastimes. During long cruises they not only take and sell many photographs of places visited *en route* to the cruise passengers, but also do a brisk trade in developing and printing snapshots.

Then sailors who have a leaning towards music or elocution find a splendid field in the ship's concerts. Pursers are always anxious to discover new talent, and the seaman who does not suffer from stage fright and can give a jolly turn is very popular. In many ships the concert party, comprised of members of the crew, is a regular feature of the concert programmes.

And so to bed. The time is midnight. And while one sleeps through the darkness the liner is steadily making her way across the Atlantic. Her decks are deserted. From either side of the navigating bridge comes the red and green glow of the port and starboard lights.

Below decks a deep silence broods. The shops are closed, the inn deserted, the concert lounge empty. In their own apartments 2,000 visitors are peacefully sleeping, the sleep born of a glorious day amid the sunshine and breezes of the Atlantic.

Softly down the High Street of the city walks the night watchman. At the head of the great staircase he pauses for a moment before continuing his patrol, and almost we can hear him call

"Midnight; fine and clear,
And in the city afloat—all is well."

### The Annual Spring Clean

In the chapter on "sailing day" one will read how at the end of every voyage a liner like the

*Aquitania* is thoroughly cleaned from stem to stern, minor repairs in the deck and engineering departments effected, and linen and crockery restocked.

But in addition to this work, which must be accomplished between the time of the arrival of a liner and her departure, there comes a time, once a year, when the great liner must be given a brief respite from her regular Atlantic crossings and undergo a gigantic overhaul, which is usually referred to as the liner's annual spring clean.

Every year the vital parts of the ship must be surveyed by the Board of Trade surveyors. In the case of the machinery this means more than a superficial glance. The boilers, for instance, must be opened up and inspected internally, as must also all boiler mountings. Certain parts of the main machinery, and in some cases it may be the whole engine, must be partially dismantled for the surveyors. The carrying out of the Board of Trade survey on a passenger liner like the *Aquitania* is no small undertaking. The actual inspection by the surveyors may only occupy a few days. It may easily take a week to open up the machinery for inspection, and another week to close it up after inspection, to say nothing of the time required to put right defects revealed by the inspection.

The phrase "spring clean" will at once give a clue to the work which is undertaken. Every one has vivid memories of that fateful day shortly after Christmas when mother announces her intention of turning the house upside down and enjoying what she calls a good "spring clean." And every one knows the discomforts of living at home during the days which follow. Everything is at sixes and sevens, rooms are upset, painters descend upon the house, alfresco meals are the order of the day, until, at the end of a hectic week or so, when the house is sparkling and polished, the whole family breathe a sigh of relief and express the fervent wish that the next spring clean will be a long time in coming.

One can well imagine, then, what a colossal task awaits those departments who are concerned with the annual overhaul of a liner like the *Aquitania*. For here they are not faced with the job of cleaning down a house consisting, at the most, possibly, of a dozen rooms, but of a floating city, which has hundreds of rooms, in addition to machinery and deck spaces. Because they have read in the chapter on "sailing day" how the liner is thoroughly cleaned at the end of every voyage, some will perhaps be tempted to wonder why an annual spring clean is really necessary. And again they should remember that although their own homes

are cleaned week in and week out, mother's
annual spring clean is very necessary. In exactly
the same way the liner's annual overhaul is very
important.

During the year the various departments concerned with the running of the liner are closely
watching events in the world of ships. New
Inventions which will speed up engines are perhaps
put on the market, or a new type of lifeboats is
introduced. Perhaps there is a demand for more
shops in liners, or an increasing call for more
passenger accommodation of a particular type.
All these important changes have to be carefully
watched, and when the liner lies up for her
overhaul the managers of the shipping line
immediately seize the opportunity of effecting
such alterations.

The tremendous and lengthy nature of the work
involved will not permit of the liner to remain
alongside the quayside she usually occupies. Other
arrangements must be made, so that the work
can be carried out without interfering with the
usual routine work of the port. And so the liner
is taken into dry dock. At the port of Southampton a special floating dock has been set aside for
this purpose. This dock, which was opened in
1924 by the Prince of Wales, is one of the largest
in the world. Its overall length is 960 ft., clear

width of entrance 134 ft., and the draught of water over the keel blocks on the floor of the dock is 38 ft. Two electric cranes, one on each side of the dock, travel from end to end of the structure, and are capable of lifting weights on to or off the decks up to five tons. Incidentally it is rather interesting to know that after the Prince had officially opened the dock he was entertained to luncheon on board the *Aquitania* which was lying at Southampton at the time.

The intricate operation of dry-docking a liner has been described in the chapter on navigation, and so one now looks at the liner safely dry-docked lying raised and helpless on a line of iron chocks, out of her element and undergoing her annual overhaul.

It is now that one will get a real idea of her immense bulk. For so great is the liner that she seems to dominate the whole town, her masts level with the spires of churches, her white upper-decks making a background for the housetops. Even when one is at some distance from the dockside one can see the great liner, like a phantom, looming over the busy seaport.

In the steel enclosure of the dockyard itself there is revealed that part of the ship which is usually hidden by the sea. From a vantage

point beneath her great bulk can be seen row
upon row of rusted and sea-stained plates, her
massive keel, the long lateral fins introduced
to ease rolling, the sheer sweep of her bows,
the great four-bladed propellers and the giant
rudder.

It is indeed a peculiar, almost awesome situation to be so near to this Queen of the
Atlantic resting patiently in her dockyard beauty-
parlour awaiting attention at the hands of expert
workmen.

And what an army of men is congregated there.
Men strung in cradles overside busy painting her
hull, men clustered, like flies, chipping paint from
her great funnels. Inside the ship chaos seems
to reign. Indeed, it is doubtful if previous passengers would recognise, in the scene of confusion,
the luxurious and resplendent ocean greyhound
of their Atlantic crossing. Her wonderful public
rooms are stripped. Furniture swathed in linen
fills the corridors. The great social square is
packed with electric fans taken from bedrooms
and staterooms. To inexperienced eyes it seems
impossible for any semblance of order to result from the apparent havoc the cleaners have
made.

Over the ship there hangs an unforgettable
smell of fresh paint. Dull hammerings sound from

the bowels of the liner. In one of the luxury suites, which has been temporarily fitted as a carpenter's shop, joiners are sawing and planing for dear life. Practically every trade and craft is represented. There are painters and plumbers, polishers and electricians, shipwrights, burners, riggers, fitters, drillers, coppersmiths, marblemasons, platers, bricklayers and even a chimney sweep. The organisation and responsibility for the work lies in the hands of three departments—engine, deck and furnishing. The engineering department looks after the machinery spaces of the ship—that strange world of living steel which is the very heart of the liner. The work of testing and overhauling the great turbine engines and the machinery, as can be easily imagined, is in itself a task of immense magnitude.

And here are a few figures which will help to visualise this undertaking:—168 furnaces are cleaned; no fewer than 150 auxiliary machines for purposes of ventilation, sanitation, cold storage, pumping, etc., have to be tested; the immense turbines, with their hundreds of thousands of blades, have to be re-adjusted; condensers, in each of which there are nearly 19,000 small pipes, have to be given attention; a length of cable that would reach from London to Liverpool, 700 miles of electric wire, whilst those vast numbers of porcelain insulators, electric globes, and bell-pushes, details of which are given in the chapter on "machinery," have to be overhauled.

Meanwhile, under the eagle eye of the marine superintendent the deck department is getting on with their side of the spring clean. Lifeboats are repaired, painted and tested. Thousands of gallons of paint are expended on the funnels and hull of the ship, deck and cargo gear and tackle is overhauled, winches are examined, the towering masts repainted, anchors examined. In fact, everything is made ready to meet any sudden exigency which the officers and seamen may be called upon to face in the course of their duties at sea.

To the furnishing department there falls the gigantic job of refitting and refurnishing the passenger accommodation. The liner is a lady. And, like all ladies, it is essential that when she goes abroad again that she should be dressed in the height of fashion. More than that, in the case of the liner she should endeavour to anticipate the fashions which will prevail during the coming Atlantic season.

Small wonder then that the task of the furnishing department should be both lavish and costly. For instance, the plain wicker-work furniture in the garden lounges may be out-of-date. And so it has to be replaced by gaily-coloured settees and easy chairs. The craze for brighter bedrooms leads to the introduction of a riot of colours, by way of expensive satin and chintz fabrics, into the staterooms of the ship. Modern schemes of decoration revolutionise the public rooms. Costly new carpets, embodying the latest designs, run the length of corridors and staircases. There has been a demand for an American bar, and for new shops, and these special features are immediately introduced into the liner.

More than that, however, the work attempted and accomplished by this department is at times really amazing. For instance, only a year or so ago it was decided to introduce into the *Aquitania* accommodation for a new type of ocean traveller. And so a large space in the liner was ruthlessly destroyed, and in its place there sprang an entirely new range of rooms, consisting of smoking-room, lounge, dining-saloon, and a winter garden, whilst in addition a large number of bedrooms were specially built. This alone serves to prove that nothing which will bring the liner up-to-date is omitted from the exhaustive work of this department.

At the same time, those people responsible for providing the meals and looking after the comforts of the passengers are busily at work. The great ranges in the ship's kitchens are thoroughly examined, flues are cleaned, and the newest ideas which make for speedy and efficient cooking are introduced. Thousands of pieces of linen are checked and replaced, thousands of pieces of crockery, cutlery and glassware are checked and losses made good. All the volumes which line the walls of the library are examined, gramophones overhauled, records re-stocked. The ship's gardener re-beds his plants, the deck steward responsible for the games renews his games lockers.

And even then, when the brunt of the work of overhauling the liner is practically completed, there still remains another and final duty, for, when the last workman has left the liner, there comes on board an army of charwomen who, armed with buckets and mops, scour the ship from the topmost deck to the smallest locker nine or ten decks below, so that everything in the liner presents a bright and sparkling appearance when the managers of the line inspect the ship before giving their final approval that she is ready to take to the sea again.

And so seven or eight weeks from the time she enters her beauty-parlour the great ship sets her course from Southampton to New York—a graceful lady of the sea, cleaned and beautified almost beyond the dreams of man, in fact, a veritable queen amongst her sister liners, which day by day plough the waters of the Atlantic ocean—the most luxurious ferry service in the world.

# CHAPTER VII

## THE PURSER

THERE is always a big waiting list of applicants for vacancies in the purser's department, and applications come from all kinds of people, from the very young up to the middle-aged. There seems to be an impression that although specialised knowledge is required by navigators, engineers, wireless operators and, to say the least of it, a certain deftness by the stewards, yet anybody with ordinary intelligence and no special training can be a purser. Shipping offices often receive calls from men who say "I have just left the Army or Navy, or I have just chucked up such and such a place, so I wondered if I could get a job as a purser. It rather appeals to me." That may be, but in most cases, of course, the applicant has not the faintest idea of what a "purser's job" is like. If he is told that it may be only after twenty years' sea-going experience that he will become a chief purser, he often staggers back in surprise; and when it is stated that he would have to begin as a writer or very junior purser's assistant, he possibly feels offended. Parents, worried in the search for a career for their children, apply for a position in the purser's office for young Wilfred, aged sixteen. As a matter of fact, the Cunard Company will not accept anybody as a candidate who is under twenty-one years of age.

Applicants might study what a writer in the *Strand Magazine* said a short while ago: "The chief purser of a ship as big and as important as the *Aquitania*, has to have the acumen of a Chancellor of the Exchequer, the resource of a *maître d'hôtel*, and the bland, persuasive guile, the swift response to atmosphere of a master diplomat." Then he goes on to say: "And he must be all things to all men—and all women. He must speak in the language of Hollywood to a film star, and a few minutes later, discuss international politics with a prime minister, or high finance with a great banker. And all the time he must be keeping an eye on the routine work, that clerking of incredible complexity which is necessitated by the transit from one continent to another of a thousand or more human beings."

Have you got those qualities, and can you do clerking of "an incredible complexity," because if you haven't, you will have to do your best to acquire the former and learn the latter? The purchase of the smart uniform, with gold braid and white cloth stripe of rank on the cuff, does not make a trained purser, any more than the possession of a telescope makes the seaman.

One can now proceed to see more in detail what a "purser's job" actually means. First of all, how does he fit in with the organisation of the ship? And what does his staff do to facilitate the transport of not merely a thousand, but often thousands of people between the Old and the New Worlds.

By this time, having read so far in this book, one will have realised that it is a very big and complicated business to run ships backwards and forwards across the Atlantic. The *Aquitania*, remember once again, has a crew of between eight to nine hundred, and she may carry a couple of thousand or more passengers. She is, as has been shown, a city in herself. It is not difficult to grasp the fact, that, as far as the care of the crew alone is concerned, a vast amount of work has to be done.

Not only have we to deal with a ship—or in other words, a vehicle of transport, a vast, moving power-house—but an hotel as well. Unlike a hotel ashore, all her guests stay in her the same time, and, willy-nilly, at the end of the voyage they have to leave her, to make room for others. Apart from the shipping company concerned, there are many other people interested in that voyage—Board of Trade, Customs authorities, health authorities, emigration and immigration officials, port, harbour and dock corporations. Records and documents are required for all of them. And before any ship can sail from this side, or disembark her passengers on the other side, a host of Government officials have to be satisfied that things are in order, and that a score of regulations have been obeyed. Much of this work falls upon the shoulders of the purser's department.

The chief purser and his staff do most of the clerical work of this floating city; the purser's office is a kind of "enquire within" bureau for passengers; it is a reception office; it is the place where complaints are ventilated, and where official oil is poured upon the sometimes troubled waters that are bound to occur in a ship that carries, as she often does, thirty different nationalities, booked in a hundred different offices throughout the world—including people of widely different tastes, customs, temperaments and requirements.

In a ship like the *Aquitania* there is a chief purser, whose office duties are largely of a super-

visory nature; a staff-purser, who may perhaps
be described as the general manager; a senior
assistant purser, who is, one may say, the chief
clerk, and a half dozen or so assistants. The
work of the department is naturally divided amongst
the staff. Each man has his own definite task,
though at times each may either give or receive
assistance from others, according to the pressure
of work. A couple of the juniors will, probably,
devote their attention almost entirely to the crew.
They will make out the wages sheets, prepare
the manifests giving detailed particulars of each
member of the crew as required by the United
States immigration authorities. This includes such
information as the length of sea service, rating,
place of birth, nationality of father, height, weight,
last ship in Cunard Company, last ship in any other
company, and number of discharge book.

On arrival on the other side the crew lists
are carefully checked, and any discrepancies render the ship liable to a heavy fine. One can
understand the reverse of joy that predominates in
the purser's department if the ship just misses
a night tide on arrival, and has to dock the following morning. An extra day's pay for the crew
becomes due, and nearly a thousand entries in
their wages sheets have to be altered in time for
the pay-off shortly after docking. Each member

of the crew has a discharge book, which contains particulars of his sea service, and every one has to be kept up-to-date, stamped, signed and endorsed with the man's character for each voyage. His insurance card, too, must be stamped.

Similarly detailed particulars of every passenger on board must be prepared for the immigration authorities. Great sheets, eighteen inches or so wide, have to be filled in—a task that necessitates personal interviewing before the landing-card, without which no one can disembark, is issued. Probably the senior assistant purser, with one or two others, attends to the first-class passengers, whilst another deals with the second-class, and others with the tourist third and third-class. In each class, it must be remembered, there may be anything up to eight hundred passengers; and, however pressing the other work of the department, these lists must be ready by the time the ship docks. Some of the Cunard liners call at three ports on the eastbound voyage—Plymouth, Cherbourg (or Havre) and Southampton (or London). In each case, separate records have to be prepared. In the old days, when a ship took twelve days or a fortnight to cross the Atlantic, work could proceed in a leisurely manner; but now that from five days to a week is the duration of the voyage, there is little time to spare.

Passengers and crew, however, do not demand
all the attention of this busy department. Passengers have baggage, and this has all to be recorded; in the case of eastbound passengers, many
are American citizens who wish to return to the
United States. Again, a list of these has to be made
out. Aliens going to the States pay a head-tax;
in many cases this amount is returnable. Here
again the interests of the passenger have to be
watched. The ship carries cargo. Cargo manifests must be completed. Some Cunarders carry
ten thousand tons of cargo in addition to passengers.

All cash taken on board the ship goes to the
purser's office, and consequent returns have to
be made—sales of liquor and tobacco from the
bar, various articles from the kiosks or shops;
hire of deck chairs and rugs; sale of stamps; library
books, issues and returns.

In the big ship there is a special information
bureau in charge of a member of the purser's
department. Here passengers come to inquire
about hotels in all parts of the world, about
trains on almost every railway anywhere, airways
and about tours, arrival times, and the where-
abouts of a thousand different ships—in short,
about any travel subject on which information can
be desired. Time tables, sailing lists, maps, hotel

brochures, tour booklets, historical sketches of famous beauty spots—shelves packed with reference books of all descriptions, form the stock-in-trade of this official. And his information must be up-to-date and accurate. It must be brought up-to-date when the ship is in port.

The ship's orchestra, the printers, who deal with the daily menu-cards and official notices that have to be printed each voyage, the baggage-masters, in whose charge are the thousands of pieces of passengers' baggage, are all controlled by the purser. In the smaller ships—as formerly in the *Aquitania* and other big Cunarders—the purser acts as editor of the daily wireless news-paper. The early hours of the morning find him struggling with, and arranging news items from all parts of the world, flashed in "telegraphese" by wireless from London and New York.

Very important amongst the purser's duties is his control of all passenger accommodation in the ship. Whilst the berthing of passengers up to sailing time is arranged by the company's shore staff, once the vessel has left the quay the purser is in sole charge. It might be thought that the possession by a passenger of a steamer ticket with his berth number marked on it would settle once and for all the question of stateroom accommodation. But it does not. Last moment cancellations

of passages, or the failure of certain passengers
to catch the ship, result in the leaving vacant of
accommodation which, in certain circumstances,
it may be advisable to distribute amongst passengers
who may be somewhat crowded. Passengers
berthed together may develop a sudden distaste for
each other's society, and the purser is asked if
he cannot shift them apart. With a full ship few
tasks could be much more difficult, but everybody
has, as far as possible, to be made happy. Passengers often, for various reasons, usually personal
and sometimes, let it be whispered, trivial, want
to be moved to other rooms. Some, after a few
hours, find they would prefer a bigger room, for
which they do not mind paying the higher price.
If there is anything available the purser will soon
adjust the matter.

In a ship with hundreds of staterooms, scores
of miles of electric wiring, and miles of piping,
it occurs at times that the water supply to a particular room may fail, or the electric lighting or heating may go out of commission. There, again,
a transfer may be necessary unless the defect
can be put right almost immediately. Often,
passengers in the hurry and excitement of booking their passages, have failed to grasp almost
entirely the nature of the accommodation to which
they are entitled. They imagine that they are

being put off with something inferior. The purser has to remove that grievance, without giving the passenger something to which he or she is not entitled, and thereby causing offence to other passengers who would naturally want the same preferential treatment.

All ship's messages—that is wireless messages of an official nature—are coded, and sent out through the purser's department, and one of the staff acts usually as secretary to the captain. For some time past, at passengers' boat drill, the staff attends to issue the instructions as to what is to be done in case of emergency.

So much, then, for the more or less routine work of the purser's office. But it must be remembered that as that office is an "enquire within" bureau, staffed by people who might well be described as "passengers' friends," information and advice on all matters appertaining to details of life on board ship are sought here. Enquiries, trivial and of import, must be dealt with cheerfully, even if it does mean delay in the preparation of those complicated but very necessary official documents. Complaints, too, are ventilated over the counter. However efficiently a ship is run, there are bound to be some rather "difficult" elements amongst a couple of thousand passengers who, as the phrase has it, "want hand-

A Competitor in the Biscuit and Whistle Race

An Impromptu Concert on Deck by a Touring College Band

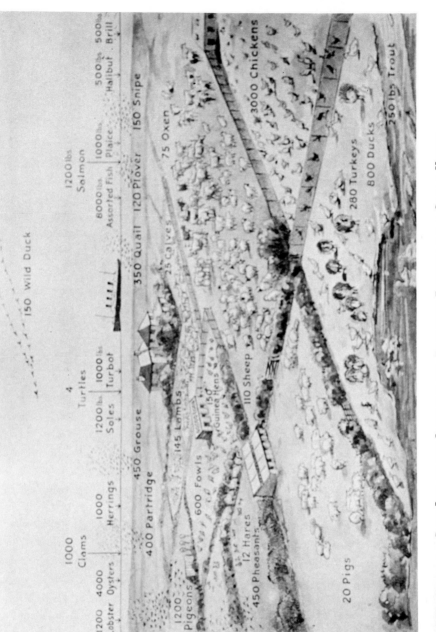

SOME IDEA OF THE LIVESTOCK AND PROVISIONS REQUIRED FOR A SINGLE VOYAGE

PHYSICAL JERKS FOR THE BELL BOYS OF THE SHIP

*[Photo: News*

TAKING THE FIRST BITE OF A SUGAR MODEL MADE BY THE SHIP CONFECTIONER

6. A large amount of labour is still required in the fire on the voyage

Some of the Prize Meat, Game and Poultry used for a Christmas Voyage

A Corner of the " Aquitania's " Kitchens

[Photo: Merrill]

AN ATLANTIC GARDENER WITH SOME OF HIS FLOWERS AND PLANTS

[*Photo: Topical Press*

ONE OF THE YACHTS ENTERED FOR THE BRITISH-AMERICA CUP BEING HOISTED ABOARD

HOUNDS TO JOIN AN AMERICAN HUNT IN AN UNFAMILIAR SETTING

A Large Consignment of Mails being Landed by Tender

Discharging a Costly Cargo of Silver Bars

THE " AQUITANIA " LEADING THE TRANSPORTS

An Aerial View of the Ship by Night

A STRIKING PICTURE OF THE SHIP AT SEA

A VERY SUCCESSFUL PHOTOGRAPH EMPHASIZING HER GREAT HEIGHT

APPROACHING THE OCEAN DOCK AT SOUTHAMPTON

A NEW YORK DEPARTURE SCENE

THE CUNARD TENDER, "LOTHARINGIA," LEAVING THE SHIP AT CHERBOURG

"AQUITANIA'S" PASSENGERS THRONGING THE RAILWAY STATION AT SOUTHAMPTON

THE " AQUITANIA " BACKING OUT INTO THE HUDSON RIVER, NEW YORK

ling carefully." If anybody is slightly disgruntled his trouble has to be cured, his complaint satisfied if at all possible.

The chief purser's private room is, perhaps, the most popular in the ship. Mr. Smith goes to the office raging inwardly, and, what is quite likely, showing his annoyance visibly. Always bearing in mind the rule that everybody must be kept happy, or if they are not happy, they must be made so, the purser will listen to the tale of woe or wrath. "That's most unfortunate," he will say. "I will certainly look into that right away. Come into my room where we can talk quietly." And he will listen to Mr. Smith, and will soon have Mr. Smith listening to him. Very possibly Mr. Smith will be so sorry for the purser's troubles that he will forget his own. In any case, nine times out of ten, a quarter of an hour later Mr. Smith will emerge, his frown replaced by a smile. How is it done? Well, the *Strand Magazine* writer is not very far from the right solution to the mystery. A knowledge of the right way to "handle" folk only comes usually, after a long and sometimes painful experience. Perhaps, really, the perfect purser, like the officers on the bridge, is born and not made.

During a recent voyage a writer came much in touch with the purser of the ship, and was able to admire his diplomacy and his geniality on many occasions. In the course of that voyage the following were just a few of the jobs that came the purser's way: refusing the services of a lady who wanted to sing at the concert, but could not be allowed to do so without causing intense discomfort to every musical ear on board; settling a quarrel that had arisen between a husband and wife, at the request of the former; preparing a speech for a very prominent passenger who was taking the chair at a function to be held the same evening; adjudicating in an argument that had developed between two passengers and that threatened to lead to "trial by combat"; breaking to a lady tragic news of her bereavement just received by wireless; refereeing at a boxing display; arranging a funeral service for a member of the crew who had been accidentally killed; advising interested passengers on the procedure usually adopted when a baby is born in the ship, and acting as treasurer to the fund started to provide a small endowment for the child; suggesting to a bewildered celebrity the best methods to deal with the host of newspaper men who would meet him on arrival in New York.

In addition, he talked about politics, music, films, racing (horse, greyhound, motor, and dirt-

track), literature, airships, exploration, and a host
of other subjects with experts. He was probably
the best-informed man in the ship, if range of
knowledge were the basis of a test. In the course
of thirty or more years at sea, he had met with,
literally, most of the people in Europe and America
who were worth knowing. The flow of famous
folk across the North Atlantic is growing with
each passing year, and with most of these in his
own ship, he had at times been in close touch.
The walls of his room were covered with signed
photographs of the celebrities of two hemispheres.
A queen and a prince were there, a prime minister,
an ambassador, a famous film star, a great author,
an airman, a jockey, a race-horse (this photo was
unsigned), a field marshal. . . . An illustrated
*Who's Who.* . . .

One Cunard purser is a member of the famous
"Magic Circle." As "the Houdini of the Atlantic," he has given over a thousand performances
at sea, and has been offered engagements at the
most famous halls in London and New York.
Another is an expert chess-player whose ac-
quaintances include champions in a score of different countries. Still another is an author of
repute; a fourth might have made a fortune
on shore, if knowledge of the world markets is
the road to wealth.

The chief purser's day—there is no need to emphasise it at this stage—is a busy one. Although he may do little actual clerical work, he is in close touch with his office all day. One of his first tasks is his "constitutional", as it has been called. Each morning, in the company of the captain, doctor and chief steward, he makes a thorough inspection of the ship. Five times round the main promenade deck of the *Aquitania* and you have covered a mile—and there are eight decks. Few pursers, one would imagine, can afford to be very fat men! Or if they are, will not retain their adiposity for long. In the course of the day he visits most parts of the ship again, particularly when meals are being served. One day he will be arranging the ship's concert—a labour of love, as the proceeds are given to seamen's charities, and often a sum of a hundred, sometimes of several hundred, pounds is collected. He will organise—and often preside over a committee to handle all kinds of deck games. One evening a special carnival ball will be given; on another a *diner* or *thé dansant* takes place. Swimming gala, a cabaret show in which passengers "star," boxing exhibitions, horse-racing games on deck, all require organisation. Not very long ago treasure hunts were staged—one, in which many well-known society folk took part, led the

competitors up and down the ship for over four
miles. Starting on the boat-deck clad in furs,
they were only too glad to shed everything but
"the irreducible minimum" by the time they
arrived at one of the smoking-room coal-scuttles
where the treasure was eventually discovered.
On Sundays, in the oft-times unavoidable absence
of the Captain, he takes divine service.

Take a brief glimpse at another day—rather
a bad day, perhaps—in a purser's life, by board-
ing one of the big Cunarders when she arrives
about six o'clock in the morning in Plymouth
Harbour from New York. The ship has probably been gaily active until a few hours previously.
The last night of a voyage means, in many cases,
farewell parties. People sit up talking until well
after midnight. Someone, then, remembers that
the clock goes forward another hour, and that
instead of being one o'clock it is now two, and
little time remains for sleep. People disappear
to their rooms. In the meantime work in the
purser's office goes on. All these documents
must be completed by the time the tender comes
alongside. If the ship is very full it may mean
working most of the night. There is a rattle
as the anchor drops, and a quarter of an hour
later there come on board a host of folk from the
shore—Customs, Board of Trade, port doctors,

immigration officials, Cunard office staff, railway, travel agency, hotel representatives, friends meeting passengers, newspaper boys, reporters, photographers. Some want information, some want various documents. For fifteen minutes the purser's office looks as if a miniature riot is going on, for everybody wants attention at once. Gradually most of the shore-folk scatter about the ship. In an hour's time the tender leaves. The pursers —and other members of the ship's company— take a deep breath. They get their second wind. In just over four hours the ship is inside Cherbourg breakwater. Tenders disgorge another host. More documents, more inquiries, more farewells. Another deep breath, and the liner moves out into the Channel again, bound for Southampton. Five hours later she is fast alongside the quay there. Up the gangway streams a third host. For another hour the bustle goes on. The passengers leave. The purser's staff take a further deep breath, and think about the pay-off of the men. Long after the boat train has reached London, and many of the passengers are safely home, the purser's staff locks up the office. The purser says "Jolly good trip that—nice lot of people." The staff-purser says "Well, I ought to be getting my own ship before long." The senior assistant-purser probably emits a "Phew!

That's that!" The juniors lament the fact that
there seems to be more work each successive
voyage, less spare time in port, and wonder why
they ever went to sea. About three days later
they sail West again and smilingly answer the
same questions and arrange those broad and
lengthy documents that heartless official bodies
require to be filled up in detail, voyage after
voyage. During the voyage, at headquarters
ashore, a few more names go down on the waiting-
list and more people come in and say they think
a purser's job would just about suit them. Would
they suit it?

# CHAPTER VIII

## CATERING AND STEWARDS

As everyone knows, ships' supplies in the early days of the windjammers were a source of sarcastic merriment, even to the unfortunate crews who had their digestions ruined by them. The ship's cook usually had the doubtfully complimentary title of "Slush" or the "Doctor", and carried out his equally doubtful operations in the galley or "caboose ". The hungry crew invented quaint and picturesque names for the doubtful messes served out to them. "Dandyfunk" a dish of powdered biscuit and molasses they regarded as a welcome alternative to the monotonous round of hard tack or salt junk. Another comparatively tempting concoction had the picturesque name of "lobscouse" and consisted of a stew made of broken biscuit, potatoes and salt meat. Black coffee sweetened with molasses or "water bewitched", a graphic description of an unrecognisable form of tea, are examples of what the "Doctor" could produce in the way of drinks. It is not to be wondered at that alcohol in almost any form was so obviously more in demand. And when you consider the cramped conditions on the ships, and the lack of even elementary ideas of cleanliness, it is not surprising to read stories of the crew in some cases only daring to eat their food at night, in order that they might avoid the unpleasantness of seeing weevils or other pests in it.

Although many people still contend that much of the glory has departed from life at sea since the passing of the sailing ship, there is no doubt that, even from the early days of steamers, conditions were much improved both for passengers and crew. When Charles Dickens crossed in the *Britannia*, the first Cunarder, and the pioneer of regular steam navigation across the Atlantic, the lively description he gives in his "American Notes" shows that at any rate, there was no shortage of supplies in those early days. "Knots of people stood upon the wharf," he says, "gazing with a kind of dread delight on the far-famed fast American steamer and one party of men were 'taking in the milk,' or, in other words, getting the cow on board, and another was filling the ice-house to the very throat with fresh provisions, with butcher's meat, gardener's stuff, sucking pigs, calves' heads in scores, beef, veal, and pork and poultry out of all proportion." Elsewhere he describes how "at one, a bell rings, and a stewardess comes down with a steaming dish of baked potatoes and another of roasted apples, and plates of pig's face, cold ham, salt beef, or perhaps a smoking mess of rare hot collops." Later on there are "more potatoes—boiled this time—and store of hot meat of various kinds, not forgetting the roast pig to be taken medicinally." The menus suggested here are certainly an improvement on those which made the dread disease of scurvy one of the terrors of sea travel till Captain Cook discovered forms of diet which abolished this scourge.

But the dishes served to Charles Dickens on board the *Britannia* would compare very poorly with the menus nowadays on board the *Aquitania*. Take, for instance, the time of the year when the Christmas festivities are in full swing. An inspection of the first-class dining-room before sailing would reveal many of the good things set aside for the entertainment of the passengers. On one large table is arrayed a wonderful display of the choicest collation of game, poultry and galantines, all garnished and decorated in a tempting way. In the centre of the huge dining-saloon, standing on the lower floor and reaching up into the dome, is a vast Christmas tree, gaily decorated with all manner of Christmas surprises. Everything served on the ship is a masterpiece of the chef's art, and there is everything in the way of equipment that you can imagine. If one were to go along to the kitchens, one would be astonished at the shining copper utensils and scrupulous cleanliness. Pantries would be found consisting of a whole series of compartments specially fitted for the serving of food. In the dry groceries store are concealed tea from India, coffee from Brazil and Mexico, jams of reputed manufacturers, oil from Italy, spices from the West Indies and French canned vegetables. On visiting the storage chambers there would be found separate refrigerators for the storage of meats, fruit, vegetables, poultry, bacon, cheese, milk. Each of these refrigerators is kept at a temperature to suit the particular product, and ensures the condition being exactly right in each case. Separate refrigerators and storerooms are provided for the storage of the choicest wines, spirits and liqueurs, which are fully capable of supplying the demands of a wine list which vies with the finest hotels ashore.

A brief selection of the fruit alone will give a good idea of how products are collected from all over the world to satisfy the demands of the passengers. There are English-grown muscat and Colmar grapes, and peaches carefully packed in baskets, apples from Oregon, oranges from Florida and California and the Cape, honeydew melons, casabas and strange exotic melons from Cuba. And lest one should think that the passengers are to exist solely on food which would delight a Sultan in the Arabian Nights, there will be found every variety of vegetable in season, including spring onions and tons of potatoes stored away in separate stores.

The secrets of the ship's milk and cream supply are revealed in a spotless dairy. Only fresh milk and cream are used throughout the voyage, and such a supply, of course, necessitates elaborate cold storage. The net storage in the main cooling chambers of the *Aquitania* is over 18,000 ft.

Leaving the cold storage rooms and the dairy one may make a tour of the ship's kitchens, which consist of quite a number of separate rooms, each of which is dedicated to some special branch of cookery. Here one will be fascinated by a wonderful collection of machines for lightening labour and saving time in order to cope with the huge numbers on board that require to be fed. In the bakehouse the great steel arm of a dough machine is kneading up sacks of flour at seven-minute intervals. The machine for making the daily batches of rolls looks rather like an old-fashioned griddle of iron. A layer of dough is placed on this, pounded with a heavy press and at the same time divided in such a way that when the batch on each griddle plate is cooked, the rolls are exactly to shape and require only a light touch to separate from one another. A spray inside the oven ensures that just the right amount of steam reaches them to secure the glossy brown surface which makes them so much more tempting on the breakfast table.

In the corner of another room we shall find a machine for producing toast in endless quantities. And here is another gadget which a busy housewife would dearly love to have in her kitchen—an automatic egg-boiler, which can be adjusted to two, three or five minutes as the case may be. If the cook turns the lever to No. 3 he can then go off to another job secure in the knowledge that at the end of three minutes the egg will automatically come out of the water and be awaiting his return. Or one may prefer to watch an enormous churn-like machine called a "Cornhill," which swirls round a thousand or more helpless potatoes and dumps them all out clean, peeled and all ready for cooking. More delicate is the work of an apple parer which automatically adjusts the size of its mechanical "hand" to hold the particular kind of apple, then continues to peel and core it, and finally throws out the core on one side and the apple on the other. There is also a machine for extracting the cores from grapefruit, and an electric device for extracting the juice from lemons and oranges.

Washing up is always an unpopular business, but in a modern liner, the vast number of plates to be dealt with are handled quite simply with another gadget which can wash at the rate of 2,000 plates an hour. There is also a burnishing machine to deal with the silver. This is cylindrical in shape and filled with steel dust. It is fed with hot water and a little plate powder, and can convert 400 forks to dazzling brightness in the space of twenty minutes, dealing as rapidly with large flat dishes.

The mere existence of all these machines will show the need for handling vast quantities of stores in the shortest time possible. One can now go ashore and get some idea of what goes on behind the scenes before a great liner sails with its complement of three to four thousand souls across the ocean, and remember that catering for a liner is quite a different proposition from catering for an hotel. If the hotel manager has an unexpectedly heavy rush of visitors over the week-end he has only to ring up a convenient store just down the street, place an urgent order for immediate delivery and the problem is solved. Not so, however, with the ship's stewards and other officials who have to cater for a liner's population. Everything has to be completed before the voyage, and this can only be carried out by perfect organisation.

The *Aquitania* usually arrives in her English home port on Wednesday, and sails again on Saturdays, giving two clear days in port. Immediately before the passengers have been landed the bedroom stewards search all rooms for passengers' belongings that may have been left behind by mistake, handing in to the purser's office anything found, or, if nothing is found, signing a card to that effect, which is filed in the chief steward's office. All beds are then stripped, and the linen soiled during the voyage—this usually numbers about 100,000 pieces—is landed and sent to the laundry.

All kitchen utensils are collected, inspected, and where necessary sent for repair. Surplus stores in the store-rooms, refrigerators and bars, are carefully checked, and the rooms thoroughly cleaned out. All empty packages and bottles are collected for return to the various suppliers. The interior of the ship is then washed out. With the exception of the watchmen the men are mustered, given their pay and sent home.

The next morning (Thursday) at 8 o'clock those members of the department who are not on leave answer the roll call, and are detailed off for their various duties, which include cleaning and preparing all passenger accommodation, cleaning silverware, cutlery, and glass, and generally attending to the storing of the ship. The company's stocktaker takes stocks of linen, crockery glassware, and all working utensils. The size of the undertaking may be judged from the fact that 100,000 pieces of earthenware, china and glass and 26,000 pieces of silver, are involved. At 11 o'clock in the morning all hands undergo a thorough medical inspection, and any failing to come up to the required standard are replaced.

During the day the crew is re-signed for the next voyage. On the Friday general cleaning up is again in progress throughout the vessel, and the taking on of fresh stores and the necessary barkeepers' stock.

The company's shore officials also pay a visit of inspection to the steamer, and see that everything is in good order and that cleanliness abounds. Men are detailed to carry the clean linen on board, bedroom stewards make up the beds, butchers cut up meat and dress poultry, the bakers' ovens are set and the first batch of bread baked. Fresh stores are received, and examined, weighed and counted, on the dockside before being put on board. It would take too long to give a full list of the amount of food which is required in order to feed 3,000 passengers and 900 crew for one voyage, but these are just a few items:—25 calves, 75 oxen, 145 lambs, 20 pigs, 110 sheep, 10,000 oysters, 1,200 lobsters, 4 turtles, 3,000 spring and roasting chickens, 500 ducklings, 280 turkeys, 450 brace of grouse, 450 brace of partridges, 450 brace of pheasants, 1,200 Bordeaux pigeons, 1,000 quails, 1,800 tins of sardines, 200 boxes of apples, 200 boxes of oranges, 600 melons, 60 boxes of peaches, 300 bottles of sauces, 700 tins of assorted biscuits, 25 tons of potatoes, 1,700 quarts of fresh cream, 2,000 gallons of fresh milk, 1,800 pounds of sausages, 15,000 pounds assorted fresh fish, and 60,000 eggs, to say nothing of the choicest seasonable delicacies to suit all palates.

Of course the gauging of the quantity of food required for the voyage has something more than mere guesswork behind it. This is the way the housekeeping arrangements work on a big liner. The operating departments in the Head Office advise the shore superintendent of the numbers of passengers for the purpose of deciding what orders are to be sent out to the chief suppliers, and the goods arrive the day appointed. They are carefully examined, not only by the Chief Steward personally, accompanied by his principal assistants and the storekeepers who assist in checking them into the ship, but also by one of the superintendent caterers and checkers. Anything that appears to be inferior quality and below the standard which the company expects its suppliers to maintain is rejected. There is thus a careful check on both quality and quantity.

Incidentally, it is a curious survival of old-time usage that the stores supplied to a vessel of the *Aquitania* type should, according to Government regulations, also require to be surveyed by the Board of Trade officials. Yet such is the case. The reason, no doubt, is that through carrying passengers of the emigrant class the Board of Trade regulations must be applied. A certificate that everything is in order, signed by the

competent Board of Trade authority, must
be handed to the company before the vessel
can proceed on her voyage. The steamer
ticket also contains a list of food prescribed
by the Board of Trade to be given to
emigrants.

Returning now to the steward's department, one
may get some idea of how it is organised. The
staff is under the sole charge of the chief steward,
who must be a man of long experience. Next under
him is an assistant chief steward, and a second
steward, who is mainly responsible for looking after
the working arrangements of the staff. Their
duties are probably much more varied than would
be imagined. First of all, there is the kitchen staff
which numbers about a hundred men who are under
the control of the senior chef, a white-garbed expert
who is one of the most highly paid officials in the
ship. Then there is the pantry staff on whom
depends to a great extent the swift and smooth-
running service to all classes, and a large staff of
skilled waiters who actually serve the meals to the
passengers. The bedroom stewards form another
important section of the department, and this
section also includes about thirty stewardesses.
Including the butchers, bakers and confectioners,
librarians, gymnastic instructors, bath and lift
attendants, and the ship's gardener, the grand total

of the stewards' department amounts to about six hundred and fifty persons.

The *Aquitania* carries four classes of passengers, first, second, tourist third cabin and third. While the chief steward is in charge of the running of the department as a whole, he cannot naturally be always available in every part of the vessel. To assist him in supervising the other classes, there are officials rated as chief second class steward. chief tourist third cabin steward, and chief third class steward, and these officials supervise the departmental arrangements and the wants of the passengers in their respective departments. The chief steward himself visits all parts of the ship daily, and especially at meal times, while the heads of the respective sections regularly report to him how things are going on, and if there is anything of an exceptional nature requiring attention.

The system as far as possible, one of subdivision and devolution. The head of each section is made responsible for the working of his section. This makes for efficiency, each one vieing to see that everything works well as far as he is concerned, with the result that all the parts fit into one another, and a smooth and well-oiled organisation is brought about.

The chief steward is responsible for drawing

up the bills of fare which are made out day by day. This he does in conjunction with the chef who in turn sends written orders to the storekeeper, the chief butcher, baker and confectioner for the supplies required for the meals of the day. This naturally varies on different voyages in accordance with the number of passengers carried. Having drawn the stores the supplies are turned over to the various under-chefs, who proceed to prepare and cook the meals.

Preparing the menus alone is an extremely complicated business. The millionaire type of passenger is naturally very particular, not only about the quality but also the variety of dishes, as the following typical *Aquitania* first class dinner menu will show:—

### READY DISHES

Caviare
Oysters on Half-Shell
Grape Fruit au Maraschino

Consommé Grimaldi
Potage Dauphine

Turbot Poché, Sauce Fenouil

READY DISHES—continued

Ris of Veau, Osielle

———

Saddle de English Mutton
Red Currant Jelly
Choux-fleur Sauté
Haricots Verts
Potatoes Various

———

Roast Pheasant
Salads Various

———

Macédoine de Fruits au Liqueur

———

Coupes Mary Garden
Friandises

———

Diable à Cheval

———

Dessert

———

Coffee

## Carte du Jour

# DINNER

*To Order :*

HORS D'ŒUVRES

| | |
|---|---|
| Grape Fruit au Maraschino | Honey Dew Melon |
| Oysters on Half-Shell | Caviare |
| Clam Juice Cocktails | Tomate Vinaigrette |
| Œufs farcis | Anchovy Salad |
| Andouille de Vire | Antipasta |
| Smoked Salmon       Olives | Pickled Tunny Fish |
| Smoked Sardines | Gendarme Herrings |
| Salami and Liver Sausage | Smoked Sturgeon |
| Salted Peanuts | Westphalia Ham |
| Salted Almonds | Salted Cucumber |

SOUPS

| | |
|---|---|
| Poule au Pot Henri IV | Potage Dauphine |
| Consommé Italienne | Potage Stamboul |
| Consommé Grimaldi | Soupe Beaucaire |

FISH

Turbot poché Sauce Fenouil Eperlans frits Ravigote
Suprême de Britt Portugaise
                    Rouget grillé Beurre Diable

ENTREES

Noisettes d'Agneau Maltaise    Ris de Veau Osielle
Côtelettes de Volaille aux Haricots Panachées
Pigeonneaux en Cocotte Paysanne
                    Bouchées Financiére
Escallops de Homard Bellevue

GRILLS

| | |
|---|---|
| Entrecôte Minute | French Lamb Chops |
| Calf's Liver Diable | Pork Cutlets—Piquante |

## JOINTS
Prime Sirloins and Ribs of Beef—Horseradish Sauce.
Saddle of English Mutton—Red Currant Jelly

## ROASTS
| | | |
|---|---|---|
| Turkey | Pheasant | Guinea Chicken |
| Quails | Woodcock | Rouen Duck |

## VEGETABLES
Haricots Verts Choux-fleur sauté
Vegetable Marrow au Beurre Fried Oyster Plant
POTATOES—Boiled New Roast Purée
Parmentier Candied Sweet Saratoga Fried

## SALADS
Laitue Tomates Céléri
de Légumes Belgian Endive Combination
Florida French, Roquefort, Lemon & Russian Dressing

## ENTREMETS
Pouding Gastronomé Baked Vanilla Custard
Crêpes Aquitania Petits Fours
Macedoine de Fruits au Liqueur Pâtisserie Française

## ICES
Vanilla Peach Neapolitaine
Melon Water Ice Coupes Mary Garden

## SAVOURIES
Canapé Wheeler Diable à Cheval Canape Quo Vadis
Croûtes au Fromage Pailles au Parmesan

## DESSERT
| | | |
|---|---|---|
| Apples | Oranges | Tangerines |
| Grapes | Pears | Bananas |

Coffee

Of course not all classes on board expect to dine in a style equal to that of the first-class passengers or the best London and Continental hotels. The second-class, tourist third cabin and third-class have each different bills of fare, with perhaps lesser variety, although precisely the same food, cooked under the same conditions which ensure equally tempting menus as the following, which is a typical tourist third cabin luncheon, will indicate:

## LUNCHEON

---

Consommé Julienne          Scotch Broth

---

Fillets of Halibut—Bercy

---

Beefsteak & Kidney Pie

---

Roast Fillet of Veal—Lemon Sauce
Spring Cabbage          Creamed Onions
Browned Potatoes

## COLD

---

Roast Beef    Cumberland Ham    Boar's Head
Oxford Brawn
Potato Salad        Pickled Beetroot
Pickles

---

Rusk Pudding
Ice Cream & Wafers

---

Cheese        Rolls & Butter
Iced Tea & Coffee

TOURIST THIRD CABIN

One will now be able to understand better
what a tremendous undertaking it is to be called
upon to supply 9,000 meals a day, many of them
consisting of an average of six or seven courses,
and how well organised the department must be
to do this day by day, year in and year out, without giving any opportunities for complaint. Another point which makes the task of catering
for a voyage even more complicated is the fact
that, particularly in the third class, there are often

passengers of many distinct nationalities travelling. Many of these varying nationalities look forward to receiving meals on board cooked in accordance with their national tastes, and they are not disappointed.

The ship's gardener has already been mentioned in passing, and some may think that they would not mind the job if it consists merely of looking after a few pots of ferns and geraniums in the public rooms. If one takes a look round the garden lounges and dining saloons, however, one will soon realise that a gardener is not just a luxury but a necessity in a big liner. Hundreds of plants are carried in the ship; and in all the public rooms of the first, second and tourist third cabin classes fresh flowers are displayed continually throughout the voyage.

The more important members of the crew have already been referred to, but there are still just one or two others whose duties come within the range of this chapter. The librarians in all classes are kept busily occupied during the whole voyage. Large libraries are carried on all these ships, with a full supply of the latest novels, illustrated papers and magazines, both British and American. They also supply the passengers with stationery, postcards and stamps, and it would be surprising to know just how many thousands of postcards are dispatched on a round voyage. The printers, too, find few spare moments for, in addition to the ship's newspaper, they have to print separate menu cards for every meal in the ship. There are also special menus to be printed for private dinner parties, and official notices of many kinds. The *Aquitania's* gymnasium is in the charge of a qualified instructor who may be called on to take on anything from a sparring match to prescribing a course of weight-reduction. The attendants at the barber's shop are no less expert in the art of haircutting and shampooing than their colleagues on shore are in selling unwanted bottles of the latest hair cream. And if one wants any socks, ties and collars, or even a new suit, one will find in the *Aquitania* the fully equipped shop of a well known West End firm, with the most up-to-date show-cases and dressing-rooms.

# CHAPTER IX

## CARGO, MAILS AND MOTOR CARS

ALMOST everybody has heard of Mr. Rudyard Kipling. Indeed, it is quite likely that many boys will have read with delight some of those stirring tales of his, such as *Stalky and Co.* and *Kim.* Some may have heard those lines of his which read:

"Oh, where are you going to all you big steamers,
    With England's own coal up and down the salt seas?
We are going to fetch your bread and your butter,
    Your beef, pork and mutton, eggs, apples and cheese.
For the bread that you eat and the biscuits you nibble,
    The sweets that you suck, and the joints that you carve,
They are brought to you daily by all us big steamers,
    And if anyone hinders our coming you starve."

Mr. Kipling expressed here in simple English the wonder and magic of modern ocean transport from the luxurious giant liners, superbly riding the seas, to the stubby-nosed squat tramps, ploughing their way to and from the uttermost ends of the earth.

And it is something akin to that sense of magic which inspires all who live in or near our seaports to spend joyous days lingering alongside wharves and docks watching with eager and envious eyes the bustle prevailing on board ships which fly the flags of half the nations of the world.

Just imagine the scene. Alongside the quay, moored by thick cables, each of which is protected by a rat guard, there lies a liner. Towering above her decks, and almost level with the tops of her great funnels, are the sheds of the docks waiting to receive within their cavernous depths the cargo which is being unloaded from the ships.

On the decks of the liner itself gangs of men are busily engaged. Some are removing the coamings from the top of the hatches, others are erecting deck gear. Then others are fixing a net which will stretch from the topmost deck of the ship to the quayside to act as a protection against the hull of the ship.

The air is full of sound . . . the creak and rattle of cargo gear and blocks . . . the steady throb of dynamos supplying power to the winches . . . the hoarse shouts of foremen who control the discharging operations. . . . A scene vastly different from that which takes place on sailing day when the liner with her cargo safely stowed on board comes alongside her berth to embark passengers.

For even a liner like the *Aquitania* has space reserved for the carriage of cargo. When the liner was built three cargo holds were constructed at the forward end of the ship, whilst mail and baggage rooms were built at the after end of the liner. In connection with the cargo holds six winches were placed on board, whilst two special cranes were fitted aft for handling passengers' baggage, light goods and mails. These cranes are capable of dealing with loads up to thirty hundredweight, lifting at the speed of a hundred and twenty feet per minute.

As a general rule the *Aquitania* only carries cargo of a light description. For instance, on a recent voyage she made from Southampton to New York the merchandise carried in her holds could have been divided into four headings. They were: clothing, household goods, food supplies and goods which might be described as fine goods or personal luxuries.

Sufficient clothing was carried to stock hundreds of American outfitters' stores. There were cases and bales of shoes, linen and woollen goods, ties, handkerchiefs, overcoats, cloth spats, silk hats, and even consignments of buttons and sewing needles.

Then, under the description of household goods, there was modern and antique furniture of every description, huge quantities of silver, bronze, plate and glass ware, carpets, china, pictures and costly fabrics. Food supplies shipped included, fruit, grouse, mineral waters and confectionery, whilst personal luxuries were typified by crates and cases of toys, Christmas cards, tobacco pouches, leather bags, steel pens and sports goods of every description.

On her homeward voyage from New York the liner carried a quantity of freight which had been sent by American firms and manufacturers. Once again this cargo could be classified under the four sections of clothing, household goods, food supplies and personal luxuries.

Clothing consisted of shoes, silk stockings and furs. Household goods included, lampshades, brushes, wallpaper, vacuum cleaners, door-springs and paper napkins. Personal luxuries included, magazines, books, windshield cleaners for motor cars, lenses for spectacles, cameras and toys and a crate containing a patent cure for asthma.

In addition, there were great supplies of "talkie" apparatus to be fitted into our picture-dromes, engines for aeroplanes, quantities of agricultural machinery and electric trucks. Some of these consignments were not destined for

England, but were discharged from the *Aquitania*, and then shipped in another liner to South Africa, their final destination.

One can imagine that behind the carriage of this cargo there lay a vast organisation and a great amount of work. To go deeply into the question of freightage would be a very long and arduous task, but we shall pretend for a moment that one of the readers of this chapter is Mr. Smith, of Huddersfield. Now Mr. Smith is a merchant, and he is very anxious to send some of his merchandise to Mr. Cyrus Smith, of New York. How does he set about his task?

First of all, he picks up his newspaper and reads the shipping advertisements to find out when a liner is due to sail for New York. He discovers that the *Aquitania* will shortly leave Southampton. That is good; she is big, she is fast, and he knows from past experience that she can carry the type of merchandise he wishes to send out, which in this case is cases of woollen shirts.

Having decided on the ship, he writes to the office of the Cunard Line at Southampton and reserves space in the ship for his merchandise, and, incidentally, as soon as he does this he is known as the shipper of the goods, whilst his goods are called the consignment. In addition,

Mr. Cyrus Smith, of New York, who is to receive the goods, is called the consignee.

His next step is to obtain a supply of bills of lading from the shipping company concerned. On these he gives full particulars of the goods, including the special mark he is putting on the outside of the cases for purposes of identification by the consignee. He then sends the bills of lading to the shipping line, where they are checked and signed as soon as the goods are delivered at the quayside. At the same time one of the bills of lading, addressed to the receiver of the goods, is sent by the ship to New York. He also lodges a specification of his goods with the Customs authorities at Southampton. This he must do within six days of the *Aquitania* sailing. Unless he sees to this very necessary duty he will be liable for a heavy fine.

When the *Aquitania* docks at New York, advice will be sent to Mr. Cyrus Smith, the consignee or receiver of the goods, telling him that his consignment has arrived. In the meantime he will probably have received a copy of the original bill of lading sent by Mr. Smith, of Huddersfield, the shipper. Armed with this he will present himself at the freight department of the Cunard Line, New York, pay any freightage costs still outstanding, and obtain a delivery order.

At the same time he will give full particulars of his goods to the New York Customs authorities, who must examine the goods on the dock-side before he will be permitted to import them. But once that formality is over, and all dues paid, Mr. Cyrus Smith is free to take possession of his merchandise, and is indeed encouraged to remove the bales as quickly as possible in order to make room for other cargo.

That, very briefly then, is an account of the handling of freight. But there is another and perhaps more interesting side of this cargo business—and that is the carriage of livestock and curious objects.

Special arrangements are made for the carriage of livestock, which usually comes under the care of the ship's butcher. The most popular animals shipped across the Atlantic are, of course, dogs, and throughout the year large numbers of dogs, ranging from tiny Pekinese to a pack of foxhounds are temporary Cunard passengers.

On board a ship like the *Aquitania* they are provided with roomy, comfortable kennels. Strict attention is paid to their meals, and if the shipper of the dog has prescribed a special diet, this is given to the dog. Then they have a special time for exercise. And incidentally it is rather interesting to know that on one occasion there were so many doggie passengers aboard the ship that a dog show was held during that voyage.

There is rather a sad aspect, for the dogs at least, in connection with their Atlantic trip, for when any dog arrives in England it must go into quarantine for six months before being allowed to become a real dog citizen of the new land of its adoption.

Then there was one occasion when a famous racehorse was carried across the Atlantic in the *Aquitania*. This horse was Papyrus, the British champion racer, who crossed to America to compete against the American champion, Zev.

Other very interesting freight shipments which have been carried to and from the United States include racing yachts, and from time to time gold and silver bullion amounting to millions of pounds sterling.

The carriage of mails is yet another branch of the important work which is done by the *Aquitania*. And in this connection it is rather interesting to note that the very first Cunard liner, the *Britannia*, was built to fulfil the contract which the founders of the Cunard Line had made with the British Government for the regular carriage of mails across the Atlantic ocean.

Of course the number of packages carried in the *Britannia* was very small compared with those carried in the *Aquitania*. Indeed, on this latter ship there is a special room allocated for the stowage of mail. And at those times of the year like Christmas and Easter, when the post between the two countries is exceptionally heavy, additional room has to be found in one of the liner's holds for these extra bags.

Every precaution is taken to ensure that the mails will be safely delivered either to the postal authorities in New York or Southampton.

When the *Aquitania* is sailing from Southampton the mail is brought down from London in a special van attached to the boat train. Every bag and package is carefully checked by officials of the Post Office before being finally swung on board ship and stowed under lock and key in the mail room. The second officer of the ship is responsible for the mails during the voyage. He makes daily visits to the room and examines the bags to see if they are intact. He also is responsible for seeing that the mails are safely delivered to the postal authorities in New York.

There is no doubt that this is one of the most romantic rooms in the liner. Filled with bags containing letters and parcels sent by every kind and type of person in the world to hundreds of thousands of people living in the United States, if the walls of the room could speak they would reveal a thousand and one interesting, romantic, humorous or tragic facts hidden by the protecting envelopes in which the letters are hidden.

Adjoining the mail room there is another equally large apartment. This has been specially reserved for the storage of baggage belonging to travellers in the ship. For when a passenger books his passage he will find that he is only allowed to take a limited amount of baggage into his cabin. The remainder of his trunks are labelled "not wanted on voyage," and stowed in the baggage room of the ship. During the height of the busy Atlantic season the quantity of baggage which rests in this room is enormous. Practically every passenger carries four or five pieces of luggage, so that when the *Aquitania* makes a trip with over 2,500 passengers something like 10,000 boxes and trunks are stowed in this room.

In the same way as the mail room, the baggage room is securely guarded, under lock and key, and only the ship's baggage master or his assistant have access to the room.

Of recent years there has been a rapid development in yet another form of freight—that of motor cars. With practically every sailing of the *Aquitania* from New York during the summer season four or five motor cars are swung on board ship and placed in No. 2 hold. These cars are accompanied by their owners, who travel as passengers in the ship. On arrival at Southampton the motor cars are unloaded from the ship. Then the owners obtain a licence, which will allow them to drive through Great Britain, whilst, if they intend to tour Europe, they are given a document called a *carnet*. At the same time the cars are cleaned, filled up with petrol, and a number plate bearing the initial letters G.B. (Great Britain) is affixed to the cars, so that within a very short time the owners are free to drive away on their holiday tour.

# CHAPTER X

## ORGANISATION BEHIND THE SHIP

IT is one thing to build a big ship successfully, but it is another thing to run it with success, or in other words to make her pay her way. It will be easily seen that in order to do this very large numbers of passengers have got to be obtained, and obtained regularly. When it is realised that one item of her running expenses, oil fuel, for the journey from Southampton to New York and back, costs somewhere in the region of £10,000 it will be understood that she is tremendously costly to run. On the other hand, she is still more costly to keep doing nothing. Her owners cannot afford to keep her idle a day longer than is absolutely necessary. She must be earning money continuously. One day's delay in port means not only wages for the crew, but expensive dock and harbour charges. It means, further, that her money earning capacity is robbed of one day's earnings.

If trade is good, the more frequently and regularly the ship can run the more money she should earn.

In the course of a year the *Aquitania* steams well over 100,000 miles, and does about sixteen round trips between Southampton and New York. It can be said without fear of contradiction that no ship has been run with greater regularity, and no ship has attained a greater, if as great a popularity with passengers. If one works out that she takes just under a week to cross to New York, stays a few days in port to re-fuel and re-victual, takes just under a week to come home, remains in port a few days to re-fuel again and take in more supplies, multiply this for the year, and subtract the few weeks annually for her overhaul, one will see she wastes no time. In the course of a year she carried over 30,000 people, representing the nationalities of practically every corner of the earth, and people in every walk of life. Her sailings appear in a time table just as a railway train, the dates and times being strictly kept from one year's end to the other. Such a result can only be obtained by the most perfect organisation, based on many years of experience.

An American millionaire who crossed over in the ship a short while ago, writing of his experiences said:

"We are never brought into contact with the line without experiencing a feeling of admiration for what is unquestionably one of the most highly perfected human agencies in existence. It takes more than one generation to erect such an organisation . . . Its personnel is selected with the utmost care, and the training is long and rigorous. The men on the big ships have had years of preliminary training on smaller ships. Sons follow fathers in the service. The line has its traditions, its self-imposed standards, its *esprit de corps*— just as has, for example, our Naval service."

This, of course, is literally true—the Cunard Line has been in this business of running ships for nearly a century, and in the course of a year handles well over 200,000 passengers. They have set up the remarkable record for the past few years of having carried not only the greatest number of passengers of any one line, but carried more than any combination of lines.

The *Aquitania*, however, is but one of many units, and needless to say behind these units there exists a vast network of departments whose business it is to control their operation, their personnel, the upkeep of their structure, the securing of the passengers and freight, and to maintain the various trades, and make the successful dispatching of the ship a possibility.

It must be borne in mind that every department on board the ship has its counterpart and chief on shore. This department keeps in the closest touch with everything that is going on in the ship. It corrects faults when they appear, it deals with complaints, it makes such improvements as the progress of science may offer, it incorporates innovations where experience has shown them to be desirable. During the ship's stay in port this co-operation between ship and shore is constant; and it is only by this co-operation that the greatest efficiency can be maintained.

With everything that is going on the management is conversant. On sailing day the manager will see the captain and chief officers of the ship and the heads of various departments, and will make a brief inspection of the ship. When the last train arrives he will welcome the most important passengers. An ambassador, for example, will be introduced to the captain by him. The greatest compliment that can be paid to any passenger aboard ship is for the captain to receive him in his own room. For the time being the captain is the king, or president, as you prefer, of all on board ship; and even if, to-day, he has little occasion to exercise them, he has real powers. The manager will, in all probability, be amongst the last to remain on the quayside, for not until the ship is nearly out of sight, does he feel that the work of all those under him has been satisfactorily accomplished.

One will find that the organisation of a great steamship company reaches not only into practically all the towns and the big villages of the United Kingdom, but they have agents or offices in the principal parts and chief centres of population throughout the world. These agents are all supplied with sailing lists, time tables, and the latest information concerning the ships, and also full particulars as to accommodation available, fares, passports and visa formalities, baggage, and so on. Passengers are being booked for definite sailing dates all over the world. Some people book months in advance, to ensure getting a certain stateroom or special suite to which they have become accustomed. It is not unusual for a regular traveller who makes the journey across the Atlantic each year, to book next year's passage at the end of this year's voyage. On the other hand, there are a number of people who do not book until the last minute. Without perfect liaison between agents and booking offices, the railways, cross channel and other steamer services, consular and immigration authorities, one could imagine the chaos on sailing day. Every passenger is allotted a definite berth whether he booked in Timbuctoo twelve months pre-

viously or gave a few hours' notice to an office
or agent in London.

It is then, an easy matter for the traveller, once
he has decided to cross the Atlantic, to choose
his ship and also accommodation to suit his
pocket. And, by the way, it is interesting to
know that at the present moment the traveller
has to pay for that accommodation anything
from about £20 to, if his tastes are very luxurious,
possibly over a hundred pounds. He will make
his arrangements to forward his heavy baggage to
the port of embarkation, where it will be collected
and stored in the ship's hold for the journey.
His light luggage, consisting of articles required
on the voyage, he will take with him when he
travels to embark on the ship. His passport and
declaration form will be in order; he will embark
at the stated time, and without any further trouble
on his part he will be carried 3,000 miles across
the Atlantic in seven days.

It all sounds very simple, and from the traveller's
point of view it is simple. But behind this simplicity lies an organisation of the most complex
nature. Prior to any sailing there will have been
a scene of great activity on the ship herself,
and not only on the ship herself, but in
hundreds of towns, and perhaps in twenty
different countries, where passengers have been

booking their tickets and preparing to make the voyage.

Little people are said to be much more consequential than big ones. And so with ships. The big ships come and go with very little fuss. There is, in comparison, less bother and commotion with them than there is with the small tourist paddle-steamer. They are dignified. They glide in to the quayside and glide out again. All you hear is a few blasts of the ship's syren, the answer of the tugs, and a few shouted orders. The three thousand mile journey seems to be entered upon, as far as the ship herself is concerned, with less agitation than in the case of a small ship making a trip to the Isle of Wight. There is much activity aboard and ashore. But the quay is not crowded—a few score people are there, on special occasions a few hundred, maybe. There is cheering and waving of handkerchiefs by friends of passengers, but in ten minutes, or so, the great 50,000 ton ship has been manœuvred out of dock into the fairway and her voyage has begun.

The actual departure is most impressive—impressive by reason of the immense size of the ship and the ease with which she is handled; it is picturesque—there is a beauty about the modern liner which even those who most lament the passing of the sailing-ship will acknowledge. It can be emotional if one visualises the hundreds of emigrants as setting out on new careers, the business folk as laden with hopes of big deals, the professional folk as seeking fresh fame in another land; if one imagines the feelings of seekers after health, travellers looking forward to arrival at home, others suppressing their sorrow at leaving kith and kin for, perhaps, long periods. But there are usually fewer tears than cheers. One can glimpse the ship, as she may be a night or two hence, battling alone with terrific seas and gales, for a departure is always, in a way, a voyage into the unknown, and the sea is immense and changing and powerful and still, to most of us mysterious. But then, again, ocean travel is safer, infinitely, than walking through the traffic-laden streets of London. To the man and woman not behind the scenes, sailing day may seem almost a casual affair. One does notice people rushing about—people who, one imagines, have got something to do with the sailing—but, otherwise, the ship just goes out as a railway train pulls out of the station on a hundred miles journey.

In our big ship, however, there may be 2,500, possibly 3,000, people. They have to be self-supporting for five or six days. There can be no sending round the corner for something that has been forgotten; things can doubtless be ordered by wireless, but there is no daily delivery in mid-Atlantic, for tradesmen, as yet, do not include the Western ocean in their rounds. Neither the water nor electricity companies can send a man to attend to anything that goes wrong. Nobody can discuss what play they will see that evening; or at what place they will dine or dance. And yet life goes on on board, and people dine and dance and see pictures; and get taken ill; and the doctor attends them; the electric light goes out and an electrician puts it right. One gets the morning paper at breakfast; one does a little shopping or visits the hairdresser; or the Russian baths or the swimming pool. Life, for the ocean voyager, is becoming less and less different from life ashore, because the big ship is becoming more and more (as has been illustrated in a previous chapter) like a city, even to its policeman.

Inside the vast steel box that is the hull of the ship, and inside the towering white upperworks, is a big community of guests who have nearly everything necessary for a luxurious life—the best of food, skilled servants, varied amusements. Almost the only thing the passengers cannot do is to step ashore at any moment. Apart from all this, they are moving 500 to 600 miles a day to another continent. But that is hardly noticed. Indeed, the days can be so arranged that there is no need to see the sea between one port and the other.

Sailing day, for the passenger, is moving-in day; happily, all the work usually attendant upon taking up new quarters has been done by the time he arrives. As soon as the former tenant of his stateroom leaves the ship on arrival, a thousand people begin to prepare for him and his fellow-travellers. The floating, moving township may steal unostentatiously in and out of port, but there has been feverish activity during her brief stay.

*Sailing Day.*

In order to describe the work that culminates in sailing day, it will be best to take up temporary headquarters at Southampton and, visiting various departments of the company, follow them in part of their labours. It is as well to begin with one department that few travellers have heard of and fewer still concern themselves with— the shipping department. The ship is arriving from New York this (Wednesday) afternoon, so one's first journey will be to go down to the docks and meet her. As soon as the gangway is up one can go aboard after the Port Sanitary Authorities and Customs, who issue pratique, in other words give permission to hold intercourse or to trade after quarantine. The ship's articles and the log-book are one of the first things to examine and see if there are any D.B.S. (distressed British seamen) or stowaways on board. The next matter that is necessary is to make quite sure that the crew's discharge books are stamped and completed for the voyage. The captain's room is next visited, to get him to open the new agreement (for the next voyage) by signing on as first member of the crew. On the way down a call is made at the purser's office to collect, amongst other documents, the list of surplus stores, cargo report and the register, and other ship's papers required by the Custom House. The captain will be there, where he officially enters the ship, signing, at the same time, necessary papers for the outward voyage. The ship's arrival has also to be reported to the Harbour Board.

The next thing to witness in company with the Board of Trade officials is the pay-off of the crew. All wages due to the crew are already made out, and after they are paid they sign clear of the agreement and collect their discharge books and unemployment cards. Their voyage is now finished, but most of them will be sailing again in the ship on Saturday, so they proceed at once to another room where they sign on for the next voyage, and receive the official pass to join the ship. At the same time they state what advance of wages they require to be paid to wife or near relative. Some of the crew work on board the ship during the time she is in port, but the others are free until they rejoin before sailing. If these various necessary formalities are as smart as usual the thousand members of the crew will have been paid-off and signed on again in about two hours.

Rejoining the shipping department on the day before sailing one can then sign on any new members of the crew. When the crew is complete in so far as the requirements of the Merchant Shipping Act are concerned, the Mercantile Marine Office will issue form A.A., without which clearance cannot be got from the Customs. Various Board of Trade notices to mariners, Board of Trade stationery, pay light dues (when necessary), must now be obtained and after everything is in order, Customs clearance and the British bill of health will be received. Then one must attend the muster of the crew at which boat, fire, and bulkhead-door drill is performed.

On sailing day one must be up early in the morning to attend another crew muster at 8 o'clock.  At this the crew usually appear in life-belts, and once more go through boat, fire and bulkhead-door drill.  In the case of an emigrant ship—an emigrant ship is one carrying over fifty third-class passengers to a port outside the United Kingdom—the Board of Trade surveyor and doctor attend.  The crew file past the doctor, and everyone obviously unfit to make the voyage is at once replaced by another man.  The last document to be obtained before the ship leaves is "Survey 22," which is the Board of Trade clearance for an emigrant ship.  Before the gangway goes an official receipt for numerous documents which have been left in hand will be obtained from the purser, amongst them being the complete list of passengers in the ship, the American bills of health (through the United States Consul), the Board of Trade clearance, the British bill of health, the new ship's articles and official log-book, the ship's register, the complete crew list visa-ed by the American Consul, the French clearance (as the ship is calling at a French port) and the doctor's appointment.

It may be of interest to reproduce in full the bill of health as it is still couched in the quaint, official language of earlier days.   It runs as follows:

"To all to whom these Presents shall come.
    "I, The undersigned Officer of His Majesty King
    "George  in  the  Port  of.................
    "in the City or Town of....................
    "send greeting....................

        "WHEREAS the Vessel called the..........
        "..........of........................ whose
        "Master is................... is about to sail
        "from the said Port of....................
        "on this............day of........ in the
        "Year of Our Lord................ and from
        "thence for.................... and other
        "places beyond the Seas, with..............
        "persons on Board including the said Master.

        "Now, Know ye that I, the said Officer, do
        "hereby make it known to all Men, and pledge
        "my faith thereunto, that at the time of granting
        "these Presents, no Plague, Epidemic Cholera,
        "nor any dangerous or contagious disorder exists
        "in the above Port or Neighbourhood.   In
        "testimony whereof I have hereunto set my
        "Name and Seal of Office, on the Day and
        "Year aforesaid.

"Given in the Custom House of the ⎞
"..........of ..........on the...... ⎟
"day of .............. in the Year ⎟
"of our Lord............" ⎠

One can now turn to the Freight department, where it will be found convenient to start with

the arrival of the ship from her eastbound voyage.
Cargo manifests are obtained and bills of lading
and consignees' mail; and letters are posted to
all consignees the same night, asking for disposal
instructions. Cargo is discharged from the ship
immediately. Large consignments of fresh fruit
are delivered, by rail or motor transport, in
London in time for the following morning's markets. All inward cargo has, of course, to be
cleared through the Customs. Often between
fifty and a hundred films from New York are
cleared and sent away in the boat train for London.

Discharging and loading go on simultaneously.
All outward-bound cargo for the big ships arrives
within forty-eight hours of the sailing—some of
it until within an hour of the ship's departure.
Work often proceeds during the whole of Friday
night. On Saturdays for seven or eight months
of the year loading proceeds simultaneously on
to three ships. Cargo comes from as far north
as Birmingham, and there is much from France,
Switzerland, and Italy transferred from cross-
Channel steamers. The westbound cargo is often
of very valuable nature and includes antiques,
pictures, and *objets d'art*. Specie, sometimes to
the value of well over a million pounds sterling,
is carried in the strong rooms. Birds by the
thousand, dogs, cats, horses—all kinds of animals

—find their way to the other side of the Atlantic. Bills of lading, cargo and Customs manifests must be completed before the ship sails; and in the case of late shipments, it is often only just before the gangway goes that the necessary documents can be rushed on board.

The marine superintendent's department is, of all the shore departments, that most intimately concerned with the ship, for the marine super-intendent himself is, to all intents and purposes, acting-captain of the ship whilst she is in port. His interest in any particular arrival begins long before she actually docks. He has advised her by wireless of the time at which she can dock; he has arranged for the pilots to meet her—in the case of the three big Cunarders, they usually meet the ship at Cherbourg—and for the tugs to be in attendance. He and his principal assistant help to dock her and superintend the landing of the passengers. There are cargo, mails and specie to be unloaded; cargo, mails and specie to be embarked. Some thousands of tons of fuel oil and fresh water have to be put aboard. There is external painting and clean-ing; there are repairs to be done to the boats, deck and navigational gear. Official drills have to be carried out. The ship has to be inspected throughout. Crew muster has to be supervised.

Time of departure, tugs and pilots again arranged and embarkation arrangements controlled. Not even when he gives the word for the gangway to be lowered does the marine superintendent's responsibility cease, for he shepherds her out of the dock, his gang of men following him along the quayside with the hawsers until the great vessel backs into her swinging ground in the fairway. A hundred other details come under his eye, but for lack of space, and owing to their technicalities, they must be omitted here. If one saw him on the quayside, in his bowler hat, one would probably not give him a second look. On the other side of the Atlantic he wears the uniform of his rank. But over here, there is nothing to distinguish him from the rank and file, unless it be the bearing that has not deserted him since he left the bridge of an ocean giant for a job on the beach.

For the furnishing department, too, like the others, the ship's arrival is really the beginning of sailing day. Linen, perhaps 100,000 pieces, has to be washed and returned to the ship within a couple of days. Furniture may require repairing or re-upholstering; linoleum or carpets repairing or replacing—acres of it, there are, throughout the ship. Tapestries, curtains, hangings, pictures—all have to be attended to.

Carpenters and joiners are kept busy. Even bricklayers find a job at times. Painting and cleaning of passenger accommodation is always going on. Actually, every time the ship is at home for a few days, there is a spring clean, so that on sailing day little remains to be done but the final inspection to see that everything is in order. Woe betide the department if passengers come on board and find the work not completely finished.

It has been stated previously that the ship is a vast power-house. Apart from the main propelling machinery, developing 60,000 to 70,000 horse-power, there is the immense amount of auxiliary machinery. As a matter of course the strictest attention is paid to all this during the voyage, but it is only when the ship is in port that a thorough overhaul can be made. Various parts of both the engines and boilers are then opened up for inspection and cleaning, not merely for the satisfaction of the owners, but in order to comply with the very stringent regulations of the Government through the Board of Trade, as well as with the regulations of the registration societies, acting on behalf of the underwriters who insure the ship. During this time in port necessary repairs can be effected.

Wonderful as is the performance of the express locomotive, pulling a load of four hundred tons a distance of two hundred miles without a stop, the achievement of the liner of 50,000 tons travelling three thousand miles without a halt is immensely more impressive. Not merely for four hours does this powerful machinery work at full speed, but for five days, sometimes six, or even eight. A few days' rest and then again a long spell. And that goes on for twenty years or more. If anything goes seriously wrong with the railway engine a breakdown gang and a spare engine will be along in half an hour. But the liner has no such ready help. In her case, *nothing* may go wrong. One can now see how vitally important is the work accomplished during these few days in port, and how great the responsibility of the superintendent engineer and his department.

Although the ship is moored to the quay, some of the auxiliary machinery must be kept going to supply power for electric lighting, refrigeration, and cargo winches. Vast quantities of stores have to be taken on board, in addition to oil-fuel and water—a dozen different kinds of oil for lubrication, illuminating, and cleaning, waste, soap, lime and soda, $CO_2$ gas for the refrigerating plant, calcium carbide for making

brine for the same purpose. Then there is the
loading of the oil fuel. A big oil-tanker comes
alongside, several pipe connections are made and,
in case of necessity, seven or eight thousand
tons of oil can be pumped into the tanks in a
dozen hours or so.

From twelve to twenty-four hours before
sailing steam has to be raised and the machinery
warmed up. This work could be done much
more quickly, but it is preferable to proceed
slowly in order to secure equal expansion of the
heated parts. An hour or two before sailing
the engines are given a turn to see that everything is in working order. About the same time
the whistles will be tested to make certain they
are quite clear.

Now for the catering department! Aboard
the ship during her voyage will be, say, 2,000
passengers and a crew of 1,000. That means
9,000 meals a day; and the saloon menu often
comprises over a hundred different dishes. Indeed the unofficial rule is that the ship shall
carry everything that a passenger would be likely
to ask for. On the ship's arrival, it will be known,
approximately, how many passengers will be
sailing again in her. The chief steward knows
the quantity of stores remaining in the ship and
the amount required for the following voyage.

After careful scrutiny, orders are sent out for the goods to arrive the day before sailing. Somebody described the superintendent caterer as the man with the biggest housekeeping bill in the world. When one knows that he may order 40,000 eggs, 2,000 gallons of milk and two tons of butter at a time, one is inclined to agree. All these stores have to be taken on board and checked.

On the ship's arrival thousands of pieces of linen, as has already been described, have to be sent to the laundry, and when returned have to be checked on board. About 100,000 pieces of earthenware, china and glass, and 25,000 pieces of silverware pass under the supervision of the stocktaker. On the day before sailing there is a general inspection of the ship. Clean linen is brought on board, beds are made up, butchers cut up meat and dress poultry; the first batch of bread is baked. All fresh stores are examined, weighed and counted on the dockside before being put on board. By the time sailing morning arrives the ship is ready for the reception of passengers. Bedroom stewards and stewardesses are at their posts; the second steward is seated at a table with a big plan of the dining-saloon in front of him, ready to allot seating accommodation at the tables, other stewards are detailed to assist with baggage and direct passengers to their rooms. Certain special stores are brought on board at the last moment; and shortly after the ship sails the first meal is served, just as if everybody had been staying in the ship-hotel for weeks.

With the many other activities during the ship's stay in port there is no space to deal. The surgeons have to see that their dispensary is re-stocked; the library stewards receive the latest magazines, illustrated papers, and a vast supply of postage stamps for, often, tens of thousands of postcards are dispatched by passengers during a voyage; the gymnasium and swimming-bath receive attention from the electricians and plumbers; the complicated and expensive wireless gear is overhauled and tested; the ship's gardener, with his thousands of plants, is busy sending ashore faded ones and receiving fresh supplies.

Perhaps, at this stage, a general view of sailing day may be appropriate. Of those travelling in the *Aquitania*, probably half of the 2,000 passengers will be embarking at Southampton, and the remainder at Cherbourg. She sails at noon. Waterloo Station between the hours of 7.30 and 9.0 sees the departure of three special boat trains, the first for "third," the second for "second-class" and "tourist third cabin", and

the third for " first-class " passengers. Taxis arrive
and disgorge passengers with their baggage. Much
of the heavier gear has been dispatched to the
ship the night before. Most of the travellers have
accommodation reserved on the trains; many
have not breakfasted, but do so on the train.
Five minutes before the saloon train leaves, the
platform is crowded with passengers and friends
who have come to bid them farewell. A warning whistle blows and the platform clears; another
whistle and the train moves out on its hour-
and-a-half journey to Southampton. During that
time the officials examine steamer tickets and
passports and, if these are in order, issue embarkation cards. The train slows as it crosses
the road into the docks, and a minute later pulls
up inside the shed alongside the ship. The
*Aquitania* military band plays cheerful music.
Waiting stewards seize baggage and passengers
file up the gangway. In a quarter of an hour
they are all on board. The two previous trains
from London have already been emptied. A few
cars arrive with passengers who have made the
journey by road or by rail from other parts of
the country. The ship's doctors are watching
the embarkation; in the case of third-class
passengers they carry out a medical examination
to ensure that nobody shall be turned back by

the health authorities at the port of debarkation. Winches are embarking late cargo and heavy baggage; a small crowd of curious folk stands on the quayside agape at the immense ship. On board the last official formalities are being carried out; passengers are saying good-bye to friends. The purser's office is already besieged by inquirers; people are wandering about the ship finding out where everything is; a steward comes along beating a gong, and shouting, "All visitors ashore." There is a move towards the gangway. A few minutes before the departure everybody, with half a dozen exceptions, is off the ship. Towering above are the decks of the giant vessel, lined with passengers, some carrying on shouted conversations with friends on the quay. A belated passenger may arrive and, after a speedy examination of ticket and passport, he and his baggage are rushed on board. The attendant tugs prepare to take up the strain on the hawsers that attach them to the ship. Men on board stand by the mooring ropes; the shore gangs are ready to cast off. On the bridge are the captain and pilot. The other officers are on duty at their various stations. The last official leaves the ship and the gangway goes. Ropes are slackened fore and aft; the stern tugs pull the ship away from the quay; the bow ropes are cast off and as the ship is towed out the shore gang follow to the end of the quay, manning the last bow rope in case their aid is required. Passengers are waving their handkerchiefs; people on the quay follow the ship as she backs out into the fairway where the tugs swing her. Five minutes more and her nose is pointed seawards. With only the bow tug in attendance she moves off under her own power; a few minutes more and she is out of sight. The quayside crowd strolls back out of the docks.

THE END